SHORT MASTERKEY OF GI

SHORT NOTES ON GI FOR TRADE MARK AGENT EXAM

DR PRITI TAYADE

Dedicated to my parents

(Aai & Baba)

Contents

About Author

Dr Priti Tayade is PhD in Chemistry; Registered Patent Agent and Registered Trade Mark Agent & she is Founder & CEO of Patent Masterkey: An IPR Training and Consultancy Firm.

She is Author of books: '11th Hour Patent Masterkey'; 'Concise Trade Mark Masterkey'; 'Design Masterkey' & 'Advanced Trade Mark Master key'

She owns several CSIR awards. She is researcher for more than 15 years. She has 8 research papers with good citation on her name. She is IP practitioner from last 8 years and practice in the field of Patent, Design, Trade Mark matters.

She guided more than 300 students for the various projects during her Mentorship tenure in Innovation Hub of Raman Science Centre .

During her R&D tenure and practice in the field of Patent, Design & she realised that, there is gap between the source of IP and processes or litigation of IP protection and in identification of the correct IP protection.

Her mission is to bridge the gap between IP creator mindset to IP protection mindset and requisites. According to her belief all creators can be train themselve to identify the correct IP rights for their Innovative creation.

She qualified the Patent Agent Exam and Trade Mark Agent Exam conducted by CGPDTM.

She provides the training courses to help the student to clear the 'Patent Agent Examination' and 'Trade Mark Agent Examination' conducted by CGPDTM. Many candidates cleared these exams through her guidance.

This book is her excerpt of her core research and experience respect to interpretation of the Acts & Rules and case studies.

Her focus while writing this book is to provide short notes for the syllabus respect to geographical indication (GI) Act and Rule. This book will help Trade Mark Agent Aspirant to cover the syllabus of GI in short period of time.

You can learn from her one to one; show your interest on email- 'patentmasterkey@gmail.com' or what's app on 7276120384.

Message code- GIMK-2, to get add in her core community.

Preface

If you are thinking to skip preparation of GI Act and Rule that can be detrimental to your success in the Trade Mark Agent Exam. In TAE-2025, 20% of weightage is given to GI based syllabus. which can be easily coverd through this book.

This book is focusing on Short Notes on GI to prepare for the Trade mark Agent Exam with minimum possible confusion and efforts. This book has provided synchronised Sections and Rules saving time and strengthening recalling potential, good case studies and importantly, comparative notes respect to TM wherever, applicable.

I am writing this book because it is one of the difficult tasks to clear Trade Mark Agent Exam in India, and now the syllabus also included Geographical Indication Act and Rules.

Most importantly this exam is required to be qualify by a non -law person. A person who is having attorney code need not to attempt this exam.

For a non-law person, it is not easy to consume the knowledge respect to legal aspect and top on that you are required to go through the GI act and Rules and TM act and Rule; the candidate need to digest the legal aspect of both these act without causing any confusion in the mind.

While preparing Trade Mark Exam it is important to understand the legal aspect given in the Indian Trade Mark Act, 1999. And the Geographical Indication of Goods (Registration and protection) Act, 1999. However, how that Act comes in play what is allowed time line and what are the forms and what is the fees structure for both the Acts is real challenge? For all these answers we need to refer the Trade Mark Rule, 2017 and The Geographical Indication of Goods (Registration and Protection) Rule 2002, as amended time to time. Turning over of pages from 'Section' to respective 'Rules' consumes lots of time and energy and eventually lose the hope of well preparation.

This book has provided to synchronisation of sections and rules and forms and fees mentioned in the Geographical Indication of Goods (Registration and protection) Act, 1999 and The Geographical Indication of Goods (Registration and Protection) Rule,2002 and its amendment time to time. This book also equipped with comparative comments over 'TM act', 'Case studies' 'Solved TAE-2025-GI' & 'Mini Question Bank', including all that mandatory concepts that you can understand in very short period of time.

This book is '**Short Master key of GI- Short Notes on GI for Trade Mark Agent Exam**' conducted by CGPDTM, India.

Acknowledgements

I would like to express my gratitude and thanks to all those who supported me in this journey of becoming researcher to IP practitioner and making me equipped with the 'Registered Patent Agent Certificate' & 'Registered Trade Mark Agent Certificate'.

I would like to express my special gratitude towards Dr R. K Nair & Mrs Maya Nair for being my mentor in the field of IP and for all due support obtained from them.

I would like to thanks my family; Mr Raghavendra Tayade and Mast Shardul Tayade for encouragement and managing themselves without much expectation from myside.

I would like to thanks my students specially Ms Sheela Pawar, Dr Madhuresh Sethi, Dr Gopa Mandal, Mr Sartajveer Singh Dhillon, Mr Ali, Ms Arushi, Ms Deepa, while delivering lectures to these people I understood short notes should be there for GI Matter, so that focus can be given to the Trade Mark syllabus but don't want to lose the marks for GI syllabus, hence short note covering 'must know concepts' of GI Act And Rules is required to draft.

And importantly I would like to thanks for time that I got when I was in isolation due to radioiodine treatment on me, and due to which I could able to finish this book.

Prologue

How to read this book so that to give maximum benefit to you?

- Throughout the book when Act is said it is The Geographical Indication of Goods (Registration and protection) Act, 1999 (henceforth will be written as GI Act) unless mentioned otherwise.
- Throughout the book when Rule is said it is The Geographical Indication of Goods (Registration and protection) Act, 2002 (henceforth will be written as GI Rule) unless mentioned otherwise.
- The book is eloquent enough to solve the queries respect to GI act and Rule that are being asked in Trade Mark Agent exam, however, if person is interested, he may download the Act and rule or may keep bare act with themselves.
- Section statements are written as it is and synchronised with relevant Rule.
- The sections and rules which are not effective as per latest amendment are not included in the book.
- Trade Mark Agent aspirant shall always keep eye on latest amendment time to time.
- References representation shall be understood as explained in following example;

Eg. 1. [Sec 48(1)(a)] -implies Sub Clause-(a); Clause (1); Section-48; of the GI Act, 1999]

Eg. 2. [Rule-59(2)(a)]-Implies Sub clause(2); clause (a); Rule-59; of the GI Rule, 2002.]

Features Of This Book

This book is Short Notes on GI act And Rule for covering the important concepts, to prepare in short period of time.

- This book is time and energy savour for preparing syllabus respect to GI act and Rules for Trade Mark Agent Aspirants.
- Case Studies
- Easy synchronisation of sections and related rules.
- One site representation of Form, Fees, Timeline and important proceedings
- You will find this book is teaching you the tactics to learn essential thing.
- Mini Question Bank
- Comparative notes with respect to TM act And Rules.
- Solved question on GI syllabus-TAE-2025

Disclaimer

Some of the statements are taken as it is from the Geographical Indications of Goods (Registration and Protection) Act, 1999 and the Geographical Indications of Goods (Registration and Protection) Rule, 2002 by giving citation respect to related section and Rule.

Some of the statements and paragraph in the case studies are taken as it is by mentioning the relevant reference, so that students can use that while solving Paper-II.

'He' means any person may be male or female or any firm, company or statutory body, etc. whenever it is represented in this book.

ONE

GEOGRAPHICAL INDICATION-BASIC FACTS

This book is 'Short Masterkey of GI - Short Notes on GI for Trade Mark Agent Exam', to clear Trade Mark Agent exam conducted by CGPDTM, India.

This chapter is divided in Three parts.

A: Short Introduction to Trade Mark Agent Exam

B: Rudimentary Information Respect To GI

C: Registration as GI Agent

A: Short Introduction to Trade Mark Agent Exam

We are looking into this book to cover the syllabus with respect to the Geographical Indication; which is newly added to the syllabus this time prominently for the Trade Mark Agent Exam and anticipated to remain included in upcoming examinations in future.

A complete chapter is dedicated to the requirement respect to 'Trade Mark Agent Exam' in book *'Concise Trade Mark Masterkey'*. However, this chapter will discuss in short respect to the same, in order to maintain the momentum of study.

Let's start......

A.1.1. What is Trade Mark Agent Exam?

The Trade Mark Agent Exam is conducted by the Controller General of Patent Design and Trade Mark (CGPDTM), India. This time the Exam is being conducted on 4th of January, 2025.

By clearing Indian Trade Mark Agent Exam one can open many doors of opportunities in the career.

I need not to repeat the opportunities that are opening the doors once you become the Trade Mark agent. We had seen that in elaborated way in the book, '***Concise Trade Mark Masterkey- To Clear Trade Mark Agent Exam in India***'.

Importantly, once you qualify the Exam and enrol your name in the TM agent Register; you will be called as **'*IP professional*'**

Here, in short, I would like to remind you about the requisite to qualify the Exam.

A.1.2. *What is requisite to qualify Trade Mark Agent Exam?*

I think you have chosen this book to read that means you have applied for Trade Mark agent Exam.

If you are getting inspired now to become Registered Trade Mark agent to practice before Trade Mark Registry, India and to file TM application as per Madrid protocol and seeking for route then this is for you....

- Visit website-*www.ipindia.gov.in* frequently to know the updates.
- Check the notification which have keywords 'Trade Mark Agent Exam' and follow the steps for registration towards 'Appearing for Trade Mark Agent Exam.'

Now you have applied for Trade Mark Agent Exam and now we will see what are mandates to qualify the Exam and get registered as Trade Mark Agent.

- Trade Mark Agent Exam have Paper I, Paper II and Viva Voce
- Paper I and Paper II conducted on same day with break in between, on the centre as you chosen while application.

Before 2023, the pattern of Trade Mark agent was different.

Following is updated Exam Pattern and pls, note that these are subject to change. However, at present the Pattern as described follows will serve the purpose.

Syllabus:

Trade Marks Act, 1999 & Trademarks Rules, 2017(as amended),

The Geographical Indications of Goods Act 1999, The Geographical indications of Goods Rule 2002 and

Matters related to IP Jurisprudence

- **Paper I**- Max marks -100

  Time-2 hours
  MCQ -One as correct option
  MCQ-Multiple correct option (Anticipating This Time)

- In Paper I (2023) and (2024) there were 50 MCQ with two Marks each.
- In Paper I (2025) there were 100 MCQ with 1mark each. [18 questions were based on GI based syllabus

- **Paper II**- Max marks -100

  Time-3 hours
  Descriptive
  Situation based questions:

- You have to suggest remedy or
- Comment on the situations provided, with the support of relevant sections and Rules
- Notes

  Drafting:

- Reply to the Examination Report
- Drafting of user affidavit
- Drafting of Notice of opposition
- Drafting of Counterstatement
- Drafting of Refusal or Invalidation
- Forms

Your Answers must be supported by relevant sections and Rules of the Act & Rule.

This time I am anticipating 20-30% of weightage respect to syllabus of GI legislation.

Criteria for declaring 'Qualified':

- You have to obtain minimum 50 marks in each Paper I and Paper II independently, to appear in viva Voce.
- Viva Voce-max marks-50

You will be declared as pass if you obtain 60% in all together, Paper I, Paper II, and Viva Voce.

To become TM Agent, you are required to file TM-G and follow the procedure as prescribed time to time.

To become GI Agent, you are required to file GI-8 and follow the procedure as prescribed time to time

It is advised to keep your admit cards safely after examination it is required to submit at the time of final registration process after qualifying the Trade Mark Agent Exam.

You are still reading this line that means you are convinced with the fact that you need to prepare at least in short for the concepts mentioned in the GI act and Rule.

Best of luck!!!!

B: Rudimentary Information Respect To GI

B.1.1. *What is a Geographical Indication?*

• Geographical Indication (GI) is an indication that includes geographical/ figurative representation/ any such combination which suggest geographic origin of the said goods in said class.

• GI is used to identify agricultural, natural, or manufactured goods which requires special skill originating from the said geographic origin.

• GI originates from a definite territory in India and need to produce map of the said geographic origin; if GI Application required to be made in Indian

GI Registry.

• GI should have unique characteristics to the geographical indication.

Following Examples of Geographical Indications is taken from the *'Register of Geographical Indication'* Published on the website-*www.ipindia.giv.in*

Darjeeling Tea -GI application No 1 & 2;

Solapuri Chadar - GI application No 8;

Tirupati Laddu - GI Application No 121;

Nagpur Oranges - GI Application No 385;

Kashmir Saffron- GI application No 635.....and such 643 GI application got registered and such 1379 GI applications were received as per the publication in the Register of GI mentioning period of April 2024-March 2025.

B.1.2. Whether Geographical Indication is different from a trade mark? How?

A trade mark is a representation in the form of logo/ sign/special trade dress/ sound which is used in the course of trade to distinguish his business concerned from the other busness and it distinguishes good or services of one enterprise from those of other enterprises. Whereas a Geographical Indication is used to identify goods having 'Unique Characteristics' imparted due to the originating from a definite geographical territory.

Example: say for Good: Tea

Owner of 'Red Label tea' and 'Wagh Bakari Tea' can sale tea under respective brand name having different logos. Both the owner are selling 'Tea' and not claiming any Geographical Origin.

But none of the above owner can sell Darjeeling Tea by using their respective brand name. All possible manufacturer or producers or concerned person can register themselves as authorised user and can work on Darjeeling Tea, however, can't apply their independent logo/sign/Trade dresses etc.

[Above examples are provided for imparting instructions to pupile]

B.1.3. What are the benefits of registration of Geographical Indications?

- The complications and copying of identity and false practices in several cases faced by Darjeeling Tee is well known, which make them to file first ever GI application in India. [Detail Case study is provided in the Chapter- 'Case Studies']
- GI registration grants legal protection to the said Geographical Indications in India.
- For prevention of unauthorized use of a registered Geographical Indication by others.

- Boosting exports of Indian Geographical indications by providing legal Protection resulting in economical significance.
- Legal protection can be extended in other WTO member countries, if required.
- Not only registered proprietor but authorized users also, can initiate infringement suits.

B.1.4. Who can apply for the registration of a Geographical Indication?

- Any association of persons, producers, organization or authority established by or under the law can apply.
- The applicant must represent the interest of the producers.
- The application should be in writing in the prescribed form.
- The application should be addressed to the Registrar of Geographical Indications along with prescribed fee.

B.1.5. Who is an authorized user?

A producer of goods can apply for registration as an authorized user, with respect to a registered Geographical Indication. He should apply in writing in the prescribed form along with prescribed fee.

B.1.6. Can a registered Geographical Indication be assigned, transmitted etc?

No, not at all.

A Geographical Indication is uniqueness in characteristics of the said goods due to that Geographical origin, so its not possible to assign/transmit the rights as the GI right is not monopolised right, it a public property.

However, the law cant stop successor of the authorised user from devolving the said right to themselves when an authorized user dies.

B.1.7. Is it possible to remove a registered Geographical Indication or authorized user from the register?

Yes, The High Court or the Registrar of Geographical Indication has the power to remove the Geographical Indication or authorized user from the register.

The aggrieved person can file an appeal within three months from the date of communication of the order.

All the above discussion is just a basic information and not sufficient to solve question paper. All these points are being discussed in upcoming chapters.

C: Registration as Geographical Indications (GI) Agent

By qualifying Trade Mark Agent Exam you can register yourself as GI-Agent.

However, you may remain interested in practices in Trade Mark. Though the case, in order to qualify the Trade Mark Agent Exam, you are required to keep in mind the following 'Rules'.

C.1.1. Register of Geographical Indications Agent [Rule 102]

"The Registrar of Geographical Indications shall maintain a Register of Geographical Indications Agents wherein shall be entered the name, address of the place of residence, address of the principal place of business, the nationality, qualifications and date of registration of every registered Geographical Indications Agent."

C.1.2. Registration of existing registered trade marks agent [Rule 103]

"Subject to rule 104 every person whose name is on the notified date on the Register of Trade Marks Agents maintained under the Trade marks Rules, 2002 shall be deemed to be registered as a Geographical Indications Agent under the Act and the rules.

"The continuance of a person's name in the Register of Geographical Indications Agents shall be subject to his payment of the fees prescribed in **Form GI-8."** [Rule 110].

"The Registrar may publish the Dress Code for Registered geographical indications Agent in the Geographical Indications Journal. The Registrar may publish in the Journal a code of conduct for registered geographical indications agents."

C.1.3. Qualifications for registration [Rule 104]

"Subject to the provisions of rule 105, a person shall be qualified to be registered as a Geographical Indications Agent if he-
(i) is a citizen of India;
(ii) is not less than 21 years of age;
(iii) has passed the examination prescribed in **rule 108** or is an Advocate within the meaning of the
Advocates Act,1961;
(iv) is a graduate of any university in India or possess an equivalent qualification; and
(v) is considered by the Registrar as a fit and proper person to be registered as a Geographical
Indications Agent."

C.1.4. Persons debarred from registration [Rule 105]

Aperson shall not be eligible for registration as a
Geographical Indication s Agent if he –
(i) has been adjudged by a competent Court to be of unsound mind;
(ii) is an undischarged insolvent;
(iii) being a discharged insolvent has not obtained from the Court a certificate to the effect that his
insolvency was caused by misfortunate without any misconduct on his part;
(iv) has been convicted by a competent Court, whether within or without India of an offence
punishable with transportation or imprisonment, unless the offence of which he has been
convicted has been pardoned or unless on an application made by him, the Central Government

by order in this behalf, has removed the disability;

(v) being a legal practitioner has been held guilty of professional misconduct by any High Court in

India or by any Court beyond the limits of India;

(vi) being a chartered accountant, or a company secretary has been held guilty of negligence or

misconduct by a High Court; or

(vii) being a registered geographical indication agent has been held guilty of professional

misconduct by the Registrar."

C.1.5. *Manner of making application. [Rule 106]*

"Subject to sub-rule (2) of rule 4, all applications under the provisions of this Part shall be made in triplicate, and shall be sent to or left at that office of the Geographical Indications Registry within whose territorial limits the principal place of business of the applicant is situate."

C.1.6. *Application for registration as a geographical indications agent [Rule 107]*

"Every person desiring to be registered as a Geographical Indications Agent shall make an application on **Form GI-8.**"[Rule 107(1)]

"The applicant shall furnish such further information bearing on his application as may be required of him at any time by the Registrar."[Rule 107(2)]

C.1.6.1. *Procedure on application and qualifying requirements [Rule 108].*

"On receipt of an application for the registration of a person as a geographical indications agent, the Registrar, if satisfied that the applicant fulfils the prescribed qualifications, shall appoint a date in the due course on which the candidate will appear before him for a written examination in Geographical Indications Law and the Practice and Procedure in relation thereto and followed by an interview. The candidate will be expected to possess a detailed knowledge of the provisions of the Act and the rules and a knowledge of the elements on law of geographical indication."[Rule 108 (1)]

The qualifying mark for the written examination and for interview shall be 40 percent and 50 percent respectively and a candidate shall be declared to have passed the examination only if he obtained an aggregate of 50 per cent of the total marks. [Rule 108 (2)]

C.1.7. *Removal of agent's name from the Register of Geographical Indications Agents [Rule 111].*

"The Registrar shall remove from the Register of Geographical Indications Agents the name of any

registered Geographical Indications Agent-

(a)from whom a request has been received to that effect ; or

(b) from whom the annual fee has not been received on the expiry of three months from the date on

which it became due. [Rule 111(1)]

"The Registrar shall remove from the Register of Geographical Indication s Agents the name of any

registered Geographical Indications agent-

(a)who is found to have been subject at the time of his registration, or thereafter has become subject to any of the disabilities stated in clauses (i) to(vi) of rule 105; or

(b) whom the Registrar has declared not to be a fit and proper person to remain in the Register by reason of any act of negligence, misconduct or dishonesty committed in his professional capacity;

(c)whose name has been entered in the register by an error or on account of misrepresentation or suppression of material fact:

Provided that before making such declaration under clause (b) and (c) the Registrar shall call upon the person concerned to show cause why his registration should not be cancelled and shall make such further enquiry, if any, as it may consider necessary." [Rule 111(2)].

"The Registrar shall remove from the Register of Geographical Indications Agents the name of any registered geographical indications agent who is dead." [Rule 111(3)]

"The removal of the name of any person from the Register of Geographical Indications Agents shall be notified in the Official Gazette and in the Journal and shall, wherever possible , be communicated to the person concerned." [Rule 111(4)]

C.1.8. Registrar may refuse to deal with certain agents [Rule 112]

"The Registrar may refuse to recognise-

(a) any individual whose name has been removed from, and not restored to the Register;

(b) any person, not being registered as a Geographical Indications Agent, who in the opinion of the Registrar is engaged wholly or mainly in acting as agent in applying for geographical indications in India or elsewhere in the name or for the benefit of the person by whom he is employed;

(c) any company or firm, if any person whom the Registrar could refuse to recognise as agent in respect of any business under these rules, is acting as a director or manager of the company or is a partner in the firm." [Rule 112(1)]

"The Registrar shall also refuse to recognise as agent in respect of any business under this rule any person who neither resides nor has a place of business in India"[Rule 112(2)]

C.1.9. Restoration of name of GI agent

"**Rule 113. Restoration of removed names.** -The Registrar may , on an application made on **Form GI-8** within six months from the date of removal of his name from the Register of Geographical Indications Agent accompanied by the fee specified in the First Schedule from a person whose name has been removed under clause (b) of sub-rule(1) of rule 111, restore his name to the Register of Geographical Indications Agent and continue his name therein for a period of one year from the date on which his last annual fee became due."

C.1.10. Alteration in the Register of Geographical Indications Agents. [Rule 114]

"A registered Geographical Indications Agent may apply for alteration of his name, address of the place of residence, address of the principal place of business or qualifications entered in the Register of Geographical Indications Agent. On receipt of such application the Registrar shall cause the necessary alteration to be made in the Register of Geographical Indications Agent." [Rule 114(1)]

"Every alteration made in the Register of Geographical Indications Agents shall be notified in the Journal.

C.1.11. *Publication of the Register of Geographical Indications Agents. [Rule 115]*

"The Register of Geographical Indications Agents shall be published from time to time and a complete list thereof at least once in two years in the Geographical Indications Journal as the Registrar may deem fit, the entries being arranged in the alphabetical order of the surnames of the registered Geographical Indications Agent and copies thereof shall be placed on sale."

C.1.12. *Appeal [Rule 116]*

"An appeal shall lie to High Court from any order or decision of the Registrar in regard to the registration of Geographical Indications Agents under Part II of these rules, and the decision."

C.1.13. *Certificate of registration [Rule 109]*

"After a candidate has been interviewed and any further information bearing on his application, which the Registrar may consider necessary has been obtained and if the Registrar considers the applicant eligible and qualified for registration as a geographical indications agent, he shall send an intimation to that effect to the applicant and any person so intimated may pay the prescribed fee in **Form GI-8** for his registration as a Geographical Indications Agent. Upon receipt of the same, fee the Registrar shall cause the applicant's name to be entered in the register of Geographical Indications Agents and shall issue to him a certificate on **Form** O-4 of his registration as a Geographical Indications Agents."

Next chapter deals with '**Synchronisation of Sections and Rules**' which is automatically dividing the topics in manageable format and need not to waste your time in turning out the pages to seek relevant rule. Actually rules contains the information about the timeline or forms or fees to be filed as per the Act and Rules....

TWO

SYNCHRONIZATION OF SECTIONS AND RULES

This chapter is providing most crucial part of the study that is synchronisation of Sections and Rules of the Geographical Indications of Goods (Registration and Protection) Act, 1999 and The Geographical Indications of Goods Rules, 2002 and their inforce amendments.

As this book is 'Short Notes', only the important 'Must know' points are discussed in short.

However, the brief discussions are provided for important concepts in upcoming chapters.

This chapter will help you while revising just before examination.

2.1. PRELIMINARY

Sec 1: Short title, extent and commencement

This Act is called as THE GEOGRAPHICAL INDICATION OF GOODS (REGISTRATION AND PROTECTION) ACT, 1999.

Rule 1: Short title and commencement

These Rules may be called as THE GEOGRAPHICAL INDICATION OF GOODS (REGISTRATION AND PROTECTION) RULES, 2002.

2.2. DEFINITION

Sec 2: Definition and interpretation

Only important definitions are added, to focus on 'must know' concepts.

"**Geographical Indication means** -in relation to goods, means an indication which identifies such goods as agricultural goods, natural goods or manufactured goods as originating, or manufactured in the territory of country, or a region or locality in that territory, where a given quality, reputation or other characteristic of such goods is essentially attributable to its geographical origin and in case where such goods are manufactured goods one of the activities of either the production or of processing or preparation of the goods concerned takes place in such territory, region or locality, as the case may be." [**Sec 2(1)(e)**].

"**Goods**: means -any agricultural, natural or manufactured goods or any goods of handicraft or of industry and includes foodstuff." [**Sec 2(1)(f)**]

"**Indication**, means including any name, geographical or figurative representation or any combination of them conveying or suggesting the geographical origin of goods to which it applies." [**Sec 2(1)(g)**]

"**Producer**, means, any person who- [**Sec 2(1)(k)**]

- if such goods are agricultural goods, produces the goods and includes the person who processes or packages such goods;
- if such goods are natural goods, exploits the goods;
- if such goods are handicraft or industrial goods, makes or manufactures the goods,
- and includes any person who trades or deals in such production, exploitation, making or manufacturing, as the case may be, of the goods"

2.2. PRILIMINARY REQUIREMENTS

Rule 3: Principal place of business in India

a. i. Where a person carries business in India
b. If business is carried at only one place in India then -that place is principal place of business.
c. If business is carried out at multiple places in India then- place mentioned by applicant as principal place of business in India

ii. Where applicant is not carrying the said business in India

a. under claimed goods but carries another business in India then- That place of another business in India is principal place of business in India
b. If multiple business in carried by the same applicant in India but not for the said goods or class then - place mentioned by applicant as principal place of business in India

iii. If applicant neither carries the business in India for said good or class of goods and nor caries any other business also then – applicant need to provide at least one address for communication in India. (and here is a role of registered GI-Agent)

Sec 74: Address for service

An address for service needed to provide by applicant and opponent and all such persons who are making the request to the Registrar for further communication. Failure to produce such address may result into non processing of further proceedings.

Rule 4: Appropriate office of Geographical indication registry

Rule 5: Jurisdiction of appropriate office not altered by change in principal place of business or address for service

Rule 6: Entry of appropriate office in the register

Rule 7: Leaving of documents etc

Rule 8: Document file or left not at the appropriate office

Rule 9: Issue of notices

Sec 80: Fees and surcharge

Failure to payment of fees is payable in respect of filing of a document at the GI registry, in consequences, the document shall not be deemed to have been filed.

Rule10: Fees

Fees as prescribed in the First schedule can be paid online through comprehensive e-filing or offline through cash, bank draft issued by the scheduled bank

Rule11: Forms

Forms as prescribed in SEcond and Third Schedule

Rule12: Size of documents

- All applications, notices, statements, or other documents shall be typewritten, lithographed or printed in Hindi or in English in large and legible characters with deep permanent ink upon strong paper, on one side only.

- It is desirable that the documents are prepared on size A4 with a margin of at least 4 cm on the top and left hand part and 3 cm on the bottom and right hand part thereof with lines spacing of 1 1/2 or double space in non-script type font (e.g., Arial, Times Roman, or Courier), preferably in a font size of 12.

Rule13: Signing of documents

- Any Signatures to an application and any other documents shall be accompanied by the name of the signatory in English (in capital letters) or in Hindi.

  Rule14: Services of documents
  Rule15: Particulars of address of applicants and other persons
  Rule16: Statement of principal place of business in India in an application
  Rule 17: Address for service
  Rule18: Address for service in application and opposition proceedings
  Rule19: Non availability of an address for service
  Rule 20: Agency
  Rule 22: Request to registrar for search
  Sec 56: Certain person to be Public servant

2.3. CONDITION FOR REGISTRATION

Sec 3: Registrar of Geographical Indications
  Sec 4: Power of Registrar to withdraw or transfer cases, etc
  Sec 5: Geographical Indication Registry and offices thereof
  Sec 8: Registration to be in respect of particular goods and area
  Rule 21: Classification of Goods
  GI registration is respect to goods and particular class to which that goods belong.

2.4. NON-REGISTRABLE GI

Sec 9: Prohibition of registration of certain geographical indication

a. The use of which would be likely to deceive or cause confusion
b. The use of which would be contrary to any law for the time being in force.
c. Which comprises or contains scandalous or obscene matter
d. Which comprises or contains any matter likely to hurt the religious susceptibilities of any class or section of the citizens of India
e. Which would otherwise be disentitled to protection in a court
f. Which are determined to generic names or indications of goods and are, therefore, not or ceases to be protected in their country of origin, or which have fallen in to disuse in that country.
g. Which, although literally true as the territory, region or locality in which the goods originate, but falsely represent to the persons that the goods originate in another territory, region or locality, as the case may be.

Sec 82: Declaration as to title of geographical indication not registrable under the Registration Act, 1908

2.5. HOMONYMOUS GI

Sec 10: Registration of homonymous geographical indication

2.6.GI REGISTER

Sec 6: Register of Geographical Indications
   Sec 7: Part A and Part B of the register
   Part A: Particulars respect to registration of GI
   Part B: Particulars respect to registration of Authorised User
   Sec 77: Indexes

2.7. APPLICATION FOR REGISTRATION OF GI

Sec 11: Application for registration [Form GI-1]
   Sec 12: Withdrawal of acceptance
   Sec 84: Special provision relating to application from citizen of convention countries
   Sec 85: Provision as to reciprocity
   Rule 23: Form and signing of application
   Rule 24: Application under convention arrangement
   Rule 25: Statement of user in application
   Rule 26: Representation of geographical origin
   Rule 27: Additional representation
   Rule 28: Representation to be durable and satisfactory
   Rule 29: Transliteration and translation
   Rule 30: Name and description of goods on geographical indication
   Rule 31: Deficiencies
Comply within one month.
   Rule 32(1): Content of application
   Rule 32(2): Acknowledgement of receipt of application

2.8. EXAMINATION OF GI APPLICATION

Rule 33: Examination of application
   Rule 34: Objection of acceptance- hearing
   Rule 35: Decision of Registrar

2.9. ADVERTISEMENT OF APPLICATION

Sec 13: Advertisement of application
   Rule 38: Manner of advertisement
   Rule 40: Request to registrar for particulars of advertisement of geographical indication

2.10. OPPOSITION TO REGISTRATION:

Sec 14: Opposition to registration
Rule 41: Notice of opposition [Form GI-2]
Under this rule notice of opposition can be filed for GI Registration and for registration as authorised user also.
Within Three months
maximm extension of one month can be obtained.
Rule 42: Verification of notice of opposition
Rule 43: Counter statement [Form GI-3]
Within Two months
Rule 44: Evidence in support of opposition by the opponents
Within two month; Maximum extension of one month
Rule 45: Evidence in support of application by the applicant
Within two months maximum extension of one month can be obtained
Rule 46: Evidence in reply by opponent
Within one month
Rule 47: Further evidence
Rule 48: Exhibits
Rule 49: Exhibits
Rule 50: Hearing and Decision
Rule 51: Security for cost

2.11. CORRECTION AND AMENDMENTS IN GI APPLICATION

Sec 15: Correction and amendment [Form GI-5]
Rule 36: Correction and amendment of application
Rule 37: Withdrawal of acceptance by the Registrar
Rule 52: Procedure for giving notice
Where registration of geographical indication is not completed within 12 months from the date of application, the notice shall be sent by the Registrar on Form O-1 to the applicant.
Sec 15: Correction and amendment
Rule 39: Notification of correction or amendment of application

2.12. REGISTRATION

Sec 16: Registration
> Rule 53: Entry in the Register
> Rule 54: Death of applicant before registration
> Rule 55: Certificate of registration

2.13. REGISTRATION AS AUTHORISED USER

Sec 17: Application for registration as authorised user
Person claiming to be the producer of the goods can apply for registration as authorised user.
> Rule 56: Authorised user
> Rule 57: (Receipt)
> Rule 58: (further proceedings)
> Rule 59: Registration of an authorised user entry in the register

2.14. DURATION, RENEWAL & RESTORATION

Sec 18: Duration, renewal, removal and restoration of registration
> Rule 60: Renewal of registration
> Rule 61: Notice before removal of geographical indication or authorised user
> Rule 62: Advertisement of removal of GI or the authorised user from the register
> Rule 63: Restoration and renewal of registration
> Rule 64: Notice and advertisement of renewal and restoration
> Sec 19: Effect of renewal, removal and restoration of registration

2.15. EFFECT OF REGISTRATION AND INFRINGEMENT

Sec 20: No action for infringement of unregistered geographical indications
> Sec 21: Rights conferred by registration
> Sec 22: Infringement or registered geographical indications

Sec 23: Registration to be prima facie evidence of validity

Sec 24: Prohibition of assignment or transmission

Sec 55: Protection of action taken in good faith

Sec 57: Stay of proceedings where the validity of registration of the geographical indication is questioned

Sec 59: Implied warranty on sale of indicated goods

Sec 66: Suit for infringement to be instituted before district court

Sec 67: Relief in suit for infringement or passing off

Sec 68: Authorised user to be impleaded in certain proceedings

Sec 69: Evidence of entries to register things that done by the Register

Sec 72: Certificate of validity

Sec 73: Groundless threats of legal proceedings

Sec 75: Trade usage to be taken into consideration

2.16. PROCEDURE RELATING TO ADDITIONAL PROTECTION TO CERTAIN GOODS UNDER SEC 22(2) OF GI OF GOODS (REGISTRATION AND PROTECTION) ACT, 1999

Sec 22(2): Additional Protection to certain goods and Classes of goods

Such goods are registrable after being notified in official Gazette by the Governmnent.

Rule 77: Additional protection to certain goods

Rule 78: (joint application)

Rule 79: Consideration by the Registrar

Rule 80: Hearing before refusing an application

Rule 81: Entry in the register

2.17. SPECIAL PROVISION RELATING TO TRADE MARK AND PRIOR USE

Sec 25: Prohibition of registration of geographical indication as trade mark

Sec 26: Protection to certain trade mark

Rule 74: Refusal or invalidation of registration of TM

Rule 75: Refusal or invalidation of registered TM conflicting with a GI notified under sec 22(2)

Rule 76: Publication of or invalidation of GI

2.18. RECTIFICATION OF THE REGISTER

Sec 27: Power to cancel or vary registration and to rectify the register

Any person agrieved can file rectification .

Rule 65: Application to rectify or remove a GI from the register [Form GI-7]

Rule 66: Further proceedings

Rule 67: Intervention by third parties

Rule 68: Rectification of the register by the Registrar of his own motion

Sec 58: Application for rectification of register to be made to HC in certain cases

2.19. CORRECTION OF THE REGISTER

Sec 28: Correction of register

Rule 69: Alteration of address in the register

Rule 70: Application under section 28

Sec 29: Alternation of registered geographical indications

Rule 71: Alteration of registered GI

Sec 30: Adaptation of entries in register to amend or substitute classification of goods

Rule 72: Advertisement before decision and opposition

Rule 73: Decision -Advertisement-notification

2.20. APPEALS

Sec 31: Appeals to HC

Sec 34: Procedure for application of rectification before HC

Sec 35: Appearance of Registrar in legal proceedings

2.21 OFFENCES PENALTIES AND PROCEDURE

Jan Vishwas (Amendment of Provisions) Act, 2023 have changed the penalty and procedure drastically.

Sec 37: Meaning of applying geographical indication

Sec 37-A: Adjunction of penalties

Sec 37-B: Appeal

Sec 38: Falsifying and falsely applying geographical indications

Sec 39: Penalty for applying false geographical indications

Sec 40: Penalty for selling goods to which false geographical indication is applied

Sec 41: Enhanced penalty on second or subsequent conviction

Sec 42: Penalty for falsely representing a geographical indication as registered

Penalty: Sum equal to 0.5% to that of total sales or turnover or sum equal to 5 lakh rupees, whichever is less.

Sec 45: No offences in certain cases

Sec 46: Forfeiture of goods

Sec 47: Exemption of certain person employed in ordinary course business

Sec 48: Procedure where individuality of registration is pleaded by the accused

Sec 49: Offences by companies

Sec 50: Cognization of certain offence and powers of police officer for search and seizure

Sec 51: Cost of defence of prosecution

Sec 52: Limitation of prosecution

Sec 53: Information as to commission of offence

Sec 54: Punishment for abatement in India of act done out of India

Sec 81: Saving in respect of certain matters in Chapter VIII

2.22. PART II: REGISTRATION OF GEOGRAPHICAL INDICATIONS AGENT

Sec 76: Agent

Rule 102: Register of Geographical Indications Agent

Rule 103: Registration of existing registered trade marks agent.

Rule 104: Qualifications for registration

Rule 105: Person Debarred from registration of

Rule 106: Manner of making application

Rule 107: Application for registration as a geographical indications agent.

Rule 108: Procedure on application and qualifying requirements

Rule 109: Certificate of registration.

Rule 110: Continuance of a name in the Register of Geographical Indications Agents

Rule 111: Removal of agent's name from the Register of Geographical Indications Agents

Rule 112: Power of Registrar to refuse to deal with certain agents.

Rule 113: Restoration of removed names.

Rule 114: Alteration in the Register of Geographical Indications Agents.

Rule 115: Publication of the Register of Geographical Indications Agents

Rule 116: Appeal.

Rule 98: Time for appeal

2.23. REGISTRAR AND POWER OF REGISTRAR

Sec 60: Power of Registrar

Sec 61: Exercise of discretionary power by Registrar

Sec 62: Evidence before Registrar

Sec 63: Death of Party to a proceeding

Sec 64: Extension of time

Rule 83: Extension of time

Sec 65: Abandonment

2.24. MISCELLANEOUS SECTION

Sec 70: Registrar and other officers not compellable

Sec 71: Power to require goods to show indication of origin

Sec 78: Document open to public inspection

Sec 79: Report of Registrar to be placed before parliament

Sec 83: Government to be bound

Sec 86: Powers of central government to remove difficulties

Sec 87: Power to make rules

2.25. MISCELLANEOUS RULES

Rule 82: (A) Single application

Rule 82(B): Divisional application

Rule 84: Exercise of discretionary Power of Register

Rule 85: Notification of decision

2.26. AWARD OF COST BY REGISTRAR

2.27. REVIEW OF DECISION BY THE REGISTRAR

2.28. AFFIDAVIT

2.29. INSPECTION OF DOCUMENTS BY THE PUBLIC

2.30. CERTIFICATES

2.31. CERTIFICATE OF VALIDITY

2.32. *RETURN OF EXHIBITS & DESTRUCTION OF RECORDS*

Rule 100: Return of exhibits
   Rule 101: Destruction of records

2.33. SCHEDULES

The First Schedule: Prescribed Fees for respective Forms and petitions and requests
   The Second Schedule: List of Forms
   The Third Schedule: Forms to be used by the Registrar
   Next chapter deals with '**Procedure for GI registration**'
   You are becoming eligible IP practitioner very soon, hence next chapter is very important in the view to identify the correct subject matter respect to IP protection, preparing the documents and filing the Forms in prescribed manner.

THREE

PROCEDURE FOR GI REGISTRATION

Procedure for GI registration have several aspects first of all to check whether the subject matter of said application is satisfying the condition with respect to registrability or whether the said subject matter is prohibited as per section 9 of the GI act.

Once the subject matter of GI application is found to pass above stage, next step is preparation and filing of GI registration application.

Further more proper filing of the application for GI registration; then formal examination followed by the substantial examination, issuance of the Examination Reports with objection by the GI Registry.

Then applicant need to comply with the requirements.

Let's understand the crucial requirements respect to the Geographical Indication (GI).

3.1. Condition for Registration of Geographical Indication

The goods for which GI registration application is being made must satisfy the definition of Geographical Indication, goods, Indication and Producer as suggested in the Act.

In addition to this as per section 8(1) "A geographical indication may be registered in respect of any or all of the goods, comprised in such class of goods as may be classified by the Registrar and in respect of a definite territory of a country, or a region or locality in that territory, as the case may be."

Means goods and respective class/classes need to mention in the GI registration application.

[The classes are discussed in upcoming chapter-'**Classes**']

Most importantly, certain Geographical Indications are prohibited for registration as per section 9.

Let's see the one by one, all the definitions and the conditions.

As per Sec 2(1)(e); "Geographical Indication means -in relation to goods, means an indication which identifies such goods as agricultural goods, natural goods or manufactured goods as originating, or manufactured in the territory of country, or a region or locality in that territory, where a given quality, reputation or other characteristic of such goods is essentially attributable to its geographical origin and in case where such goods are manufactured goods one of the activities of either the production or of processing or preparation of the goods concerned takes place in such territory, region or locality, as the case may be."

As per Sec 2(1)(f); "goods, means -any agricultural, natural or manufactured goods or any goods of handicraft or of industry and includes foodstuff."

As per Sec 2(1)(g); "Indication, means including any name, geographical or figurative representation or any combination of them conveying or suggesting the geographical origin of goods to which it applies."

As per Sec 2(1)(k); "Producer, means, any person who-

i. if such goods are agricultural goods, produces the goods and includes the person who processes or packages such goods;
ii. if such goods are natural goods, exploits the goods;
iii. if such goods are handicraft or industrial goods, makes or manufactures the goods,
iv. and includes any person who trades or deals in such production, exploitation, making or manufacturing, as the case may be, of the goods".

3.2. *Prohibition of registration of certain Geographical indication*

As per the section 9 of the GI act, following are the certain Geographical Indication which are prohibited from the registration.

As per Sec 9(a): "The use of which would be likely to deceive or cause confusion."

Eg. Suppose some another applicant is trying to apply for Darjeeling Tea logo with change of women holding tea by just 'cup of tea'. This change is causing confusion within the mind public.

As per Sec 9(b): "The use of which would be contrary to any law for the time being in force."

For instance, if the GI applied for is prohibited under the Emblems and Names (prevention of Improper Use) Act, 1950.

Eg. As similar in the trade mark act, here too, any flag or name 'Tiranga' or any such representation in the form of logo or word which is related to Emblem or Names under the Emblems and Names (prevention of Improper Use) Act, 1950 as in the GI application is prohibited from registration.

As per Sec 9(c): "Which comprises or contains scandalous or obscene matter"

In case of an objection to registration based on the ground of sec 9(c), then the applicant need to prove that the GI applied for registration is not scandalous or obscene.

As per Sec 9(d): "Which comprises or contains any matter likely to hurt the religious susceptibilities of any class or section of the citizens of India

Eg. 'Jai Ma Sherawali'; 'Buddham Sharanam gacchamee', etc.

As per Sec 9(e): Which would otherwise be disentitled to protection in a court

The Registrar would not normally extend the protection "to persons whose case is not founded in truth" *(The Manual GI Practice and procedure provides this case Eno v Dunn 7 RPC 311, pg.318).*

As per Sec 9(f): Which are determined to generic names or indications of goods and are, therefore, not or ceases to be protected in their country of origin, or which have fallen in to disuse in that country.

The name of a goods which, although relates to the place or the region where the goods was originally produced or manufactured, has lost its original meaning and has become the common name of such goods and serves as a designation for or indication of the kind, nature, type or other property or characteristics of the goods. Which implies, the name has ceased to be distinctive of a particular source and become common to the trade.

Eg. Camembert is a generic term for cheese.

3.3. Special Provision Relating to TM

This topic is more suspectable to appear in the Exam this time.

As per the combine provision of the trade mark act and Rule and GI Act & Rule; request respect to refusal or invalidation of a trade mark u/sec 25(a) and (b) is made for that Form TM-O as prescribed in the Trade Mark Rules, 2017.

Let's discuss the conditions when such refusal based on GI act and Rule is possible and when we can obtain relief.

3.3.1. Prohibition of Registration of Geographical Indication as Trade Mark

As per Sec 25. Prohibition of Registration of Geographical Indication as Trade Mark

"Notwithstanding anything contained in the Trade Marks Act, 1999, the Registrar of Trade Marks referred to in section 3 of that Act, shall, *suo motu* or at the request of an interested party, refuse or invalidate the registration of a trade mark which-

(a) contains or consists of a geographical indication with respect to the goods or class or classes of goods not originating in the territory of a country, or a region or locality in that territory which such geographical indication indicates, if use of such geographical indications in the trade mark for such goods, is of such a nature as to confuse or mislead the persons as to the true place of origin of such goods or class or classes of goods [Sec 25(a)];

(b) contains or consists of a geographical indication identifying goods or class or classes of goods notified under sub-section (2) of section 22. [Sec

25(b)]"

Rule 74(1). Refusal or Invalidation of Registration of Trade Marks.-

"Where the Registrar of Trade Marks on his own motion decides to refuse the registration of a trade mark or invalidate a registered trade mark pursuant to sub-section (a) of Section 25 of the Geographical Indications of Goods (Registration and Protection) Act, 1999, he shall in writing notify the applicants or the registered proprietor of the trade mark, as the case may be, stating the reason for the same. Thereafter, the Registrar shall decide the matter after giving the applicant or the registered proprietor of the trade mark, as the case may be, an opportunity of being heard."

Rule 74 (2).

"A request under sub-section (a) of section 25 to refuse a trade mark or invalidate a registered trade mark which contains or consists of a geographical indication not originating in the territory of a country, or a region, or locality in that territory which such geographical indication indicates , which is likely to cause confusion or mislead persons as to the true place of origin of such goods or class or classes of goods shall be made in the prescribed form under the **Trade Marks Rules, 2002.** Thereafter, in case of a request for refusal the Registrar of Trade Marks shall forward the same to the applicant and provide an opportunity of being heard to the applicant. In case of a request for invalidation, the Registrar of Trade Marks shall forward the request to the registered proprietor and the procedure set out in Rule 93 of the **Trade Marks Rules, 2002** shall apply *mutatis mutandis* to further proceedings on the matter."

Rule 93 of the Trade Mark Act is "Cancellation of registration of registered user".

"Rule 75(1). Refusal or Invalidation of Registered Trade Mark Conflicting with a geographical indication notified under Section 22(2).- "

Let's see what is clause of section 22(2)

"The Central Government may, if necessary so to do for providing additional protection to certain goods or classes of goods are specified in the Official Gazette and are allowed to processed further for the purpose of such protection."

Where the Registrar of Trade Marks on his own motion decides to refuse an application or invalidate the registration of a trade mark pursuant to sub-section (b) of Section 25 of the Geographical Indications of Goods (Registration and Protection) Act, 1999, he shall notify in writing to the applicant or the registered proprietor of the trade mark, as the case may be, stating the reasons for the same.

Thereafter, the Registrar shall decide the matter after giving the applicant or the registered proprietor of thetrade mark, as the case may be, an opportunity of being heard.

Rule 75 (2). Refusal or invalidation under Section 25(b) of notified geographical indications .-

"A request under sub-section (b) of section 25 to refuse an application for the registration of a trade mark or invalidate a registered trademark which conflict with or which contains or consists of a geographical indication identifying goods or class or classes of goods notified under sub-section (2) of section 22 shall be made in the prescribed form under the **Trade Marks Rules, 2002.** Thereafter, in case of request for refusal, the Registrar of Trade Marks shall forward the same to the applicant and provide an opportunity of being heard to the applicant. In case of request for invalidation , the Registrar of Trade Mark shall forward the request to the registered proprietor and the procedure set out in Rule 93 of the **Trade Marks Rules, 2002** shall apply *mutatis mutandis* to further proceedings on the matter."

Rule 76(1). Publication of refusal or invalidation of Geographical indications.-

"The Registrar of Trade Marks shall record and publish a reference to the refusal or the invalidation of the registration of a trade mark pursuant to section 25 of the Geographical Indications of Goods (Registration and Protection) Act, 1999 and forwarded a copy of the publication to the Registrar of Geographical Indications.

Whichshall include: –

(a) the representation of the mark;

(b) the application or registration number of the trade mark, as the case may be;

(c) the name and address of the applicant or the registered proprietor, as the case may be;

(d) the date of application or the date of registration in the case of a registered trade mark, as the case may be;

(e) the list of goods or class of goods in respect of which the trade mark was applied for or was registered; and

(f) a summary of the ground on which the application for registration of a trade mark had been refused or the registration of the registered trade mark was invalidated."

As per Sec 26. Protection to Certain Trade Marks

"(1) Where a trade mark contains or consists of a geographical indication and has been applied for or registered in good faith under the law relating to trade marks for the time being in force, or where rights to such trade mark have been acquired through use in good faith either-

(a) Before the commencement of this Act; or

(b) before the date of filing the application for registration of such geographical indication under this Act;

nothing contained in this Act shall prejudice the registrability or the validity of the registration of such trade mark under the law relating to the trade marks for the time being in force, or the right to use such trade mark, on the ground that such trade mark is identical with or similar to such geographical indication.

(2) Nothing contained in this Act shall apply in respect of a geographical indication with respect to goods or class or classes of goods for which such geographical indication is identical with the term customary in common language as the common name of such goods in any part of India on or before the 1st day of January, 1995.

(3) Nothing contained in this Act shall in any way prejudice the right of any person to use, in the course of trade, that person's name or the name of that person's predecessor in business, except where such name is used in such a manner as to confuse or mislead the people.

(4) Notwithstanding anything contained in the Trade Marks Act, 1999 or in this Act, no action in connection with the use or registration of a trade mark shall be taken after the expiry of five years from the date on which such use or registration infringes any geographical indication registered under this Act has become known to the registered proprietor or authorised user registered in respect of such geographical indication under this Act or after the date of registration of the trade mark under the said Trade Marks Act subject to the condition that the trade mark has been published under the provisions of the said Trade Marks Act, 1999 or the rules made thereunder by that date, if such date is earlier than the date on which such infringement became known to such proprietor or authorised user and such geographical indication is not used or registered in bad faith."

3.4. *Preparation and Filing GI Registration application*

Before proceeding towards preparation of GI registration application one must understand following concepts, clearly.

Q.1. *Who can apply for registration of Geographical indication?*

As per sec11(1):

- Any association of persons
- Any association of producers or
- any organisation or
- authority established by or under any law representing the interest of the producers of the concerned goods may apply for registration of a Geographical Indication.
- The Applicant has to be a legal entity

Any of the above when becomes applicant they need to prove that they represent the interest of producers.

Q.2. *Where to Apply for GI registration?*

The GI Registry is situated at Geographical Indications Registry, Intellectual Property Office Building, G.S.T. Road, Guindy, Chennai – 600032 having all-India Jurisdiction.

Application or any other document may be filed directly in the GI Registry, Chennai, or may be sent by post or registered post or speed post or courier services or through comprehensive e-filing.

Q.3. *What are the types of GI Applications?*

There are 4 types of GI application for which Form GI-1 need to be used.

Ordinary Application:

An Application which has been filed to register a Geographical Indication of India.

Convention Application:

An Application filed for registration of a Geographical Indication from a convention country, along with proof of registration / filing of that Geographical Indication in the Home Country.

Single Class Application:
An application which has been filed to register for a specification of goods included in one class.

Multi Class Application:
A single application filed for registration of Geographical Indications for different or more than one classes of goods.

Q.4. How to file GI Application?

Filing of a Geographical Indications Application [Fee: 5000/-]

- An Indian application for the registration of a geographical indications can be made in triplicate in

  Form GI – 1(A) for single class
  Form GI – 1 (C) for multiple classes.

- A Convention Application shall be made in triplicate in

  Form GI – 1(B) for single class
  Form GI – 1 (D) for multiple classes.

- Power of Attorney, if required.
- An Application shall be signed by the applicant or his agent

Q.5. What shall be contents of application?

As per Sec 11(2), A GI Application shall contain the following:

I. Application for registration of a GI shall contain the duly filled Application form.

Specification, description of goods, proof of origin, method of production, uniqueness, inspection body and other details, as required under rule 32, may be made as statement of case and enclosed along with the duly filled application form.

i. Specification – A brief statement describing the special characteristics and quality parameters of the goods in about 50 to 100 words.

ii. Description of goods giving its uniqueness and geographical linkage – A detailed description of the GI shall clearly indicate its special characteristics, unique features, linkage to the specific geographical location including human creativity involved. Environmental factors such as soil, water and climatic condition may be clearly brought out. This part shall also contain the standard benchmark set by the producers of the GI. Fixing such a standard may be necessary for quality control, inspection and enforcement of the GI.

iii. Method of Production – This part shall describe in detail the method of production, including the process involved, raw materials and tools, packaging specialty if any, etc.

iv. Uniqueness of the product – This part may contain the comparison with other similar products, so as to establish its uniqueness of the goods for which registration is applied. This part may be described in not more than 100 words.

v. Proof of Origin - Historic proof in the form of documentary evidence, shall be submitted, to prove the existence of the Geographical Indications such as, gazetteers, published documents, news articles, advertisement materials, for clearly bringing out the historic development of the Geographical Indications.

vi. Inspection Body - This part may contain details of the Inspection Body set-up by the Applicant to monitor the production in respect of quality, integrity and consistency of the product as well as the genuine use of the GI.

vii. Present scenario of the GI product – This part shall elaborate the present market of the GI product with the details of exports, if any, total turnover of the product, and the activities undertaken by the applicant association in development and promotion of the GI.

B. Three copies of map of the geographical area of production showing the title, name of publisher and date of issue. The copies shall be certified by a competent authority.

C. List of members of the association of producers. Such list may contain the list of producers, who initially propose to get the GI registered and need not be an exhaustive list of all the producers.

D. Two additional representations as required under rule 27. As the application forms are digitized by the GI Registry, only two additional representations are sufficient, instead of five.

E. An Affidavit, as required under rule 32(6)(a). No affidavit is required to be submitted if the applicant is an association of producers of goods.

F. Registration certificate from the competent authority along with the bye-laws / articles of association / memorandum of association clearly describing the objectives of association.

G. Self-attested copy of English Translation may be submitted, if these documents are in a language other than English or Hindi.

A clause for removal of members of an association on the ground of not conforming to the standards of production of the goods is advisable. Such a clause would ensure consistency in quality of goods produced by members of the association.

H. In case of Convention Applications, a Certificate shall accompany the application. The certificate shall be issued by the Competent Authority at the Geographical Indications Office of the Convention Country, along with a Statement indicating the Filing Date of the Foreign Application relied upon in the Convention Country where it was filed, and serial number, if available. However, such a certificate can be filed within two months from the date of filing of the Application

A document entitled 'statement of case' (in triplicate), to be annexed to the documents

[A filed and registered GI is provided in _Case study 1: Darjeeling Tea_]

II. Preparing formal documents

- All applications, notices, statements, or other documents shall be typewritten, lithographed or printed in Hindi or in English in large and legible characters with deep permanent ink upon strong paper, on one side only.
- It is desirable that the documents are prepared on size A4 with a margin of at least 4 cm on the top and left hand part and 3 centimetres on the bottom and right hand part thereof with lines spacing of 1 1/2 or double space in non-script type font (e.g., Arial, Times Roman, or Courier), preferably in a font size of 12.

Signing of documents

- Any application or document to be filed before the Geographical Indication Registry, by an association of persons or producers shall be signed by the authorised signatory. The capacity in which an individual sign a document on behalf of an association of persons or a body corporate shall be stated below his signature.

- Any Signatures to an application and any other documents shall be accompanied by the name of the signatory in English (in capital letters) or in Hindi.
- It is desirable that the documents are filed as Annexures to Application and Statement of Case. The Applicant or the authorized Signatory shall append his signature at the end of each annexure or document.

3.4. Special provision respect to homonymous Geographical Indications

As per; Sec 10. Registration of homonymous geographical indication

Where the geographical indication is a homonymous indication to an already registered geographical indication, the material factors differentiating the application from the registered geographical indications shall be provided.

The Particulars of protective measures adopted by the applicant to ensure consumers of such goods are not confused or mislead or confused in consequence of such registration.

3.5. Examination of GI Application

3.5.1. Formal Examination

On receipt of an application, the Examiner/Authorised Officer shall scrutinize the application and the accompanying Statement of Case as to whether it meets the requirements of the GI Act and the Rules viz.:

- application has been filed in a prescribed Form
- prescribed Fees have been paid
- applicant or his agent has appended his signature in the Application
- application has been filed along with Five Additional representations
- application has been filed along with Statement of case in Triplicate
- application has been filed along with Three Certified copies of Map, which should clearly indicate the latitude and longitude of the

Geographical Indications Area.

- address of Service in India is provided in case of a Convention Application.
- power of attorney or Authorisation Form has been executed and submitted in Original.
- class of Goods has been mentioned correctly.
- documentary evidence (Original / Notarised / Attested) relating to the legal status of applicant such as Memorandum and Articles of Association, Bye - laws, Registration certificates, etc has been filed.
- translation / transliteration of the non-English / Hindi text has been provided.
- certificate from the competent authority of the convention country has been filed along with the necessary particulars.

Communication of deficiencies found in preliminary examination: [Rule 31]

Rule 31: Deficiencies

- Deficiencies if any found through a preliminary examination as mentioned in the above paragraph shall be communicated by the Examiner/Authorised Officer to the Applicant or his Agent.
- The deficiencies shall be complied within **one month.**
- If the Applicant fails to remedy any deficiencies within the stipulated time so notified, the Application may be treated as **<u>abandoned.</u>**
- However, the Applicant may file a request of extension of time of One month in Form GI-9(C) with prescribed fee.
- Fees: 300/-
- When the deficiencies are complied the Examiner/Authorised Officer shall submit the Application to the Registrar of GI for his consideration.

3.5.2. Substantial Examination of Application:

Rule 34: Objection to acceptance -hearing

A consultative group is constituted **As per Rule 33: 'Examination of application'.**

Upon compliance of the deficiencies, the Registrar shall ordinarily constitute a Consultative Group of not more than seven representatives to ascertain the correctness of the particulars furnished in the Statement of Case.

The Consultative Group is chaired by the Registrar of Geographical Indications.

The remaining members are identified from any organisation, authority or persons well versed in the varied intricacies of the Geographical Indications Law or field, to ascertain the correctness of the particulars furnished in the statement of Case.

As a matter of practice, for the benefits of the Applicants the Consultative group meeting are being held at the GI Registry, Chennai and Intellectual Property Offices situated in Delhi, Mumbai and Kolkata. The Meetings may also be held at other locations if the situation so warrants.

The Applicant will be invited to make a detailed presentation before the Consultative Group to explain the statement of case. The Consultative Group ascertains the correctness of the particulars of Statement of Case and recommends for amendments, corrections or furnishing of further documents. The Group may visit the production area in order to further assess the correctness of the Statement of Case.

The proceeding before the Consultative group will be ordinarily completed **within three months from the date of constitution.**

There upon the Registrar shall consider the Application on merits and based on observation / comments of Consultative Group, issues an Examination Report.

The Examination Report may contain objections to the acceptance of the Application or proposal to accept it subject to such conditions, amendments, modification or limitations as the Register may think fit to impose.

The Applicant shall **within two months** of the date of communication of Examination Report comply with proposals mentioned in the Examination Report or submit his observation or apply for a Hearing.

If the applicant fails to amend his application or submit his observations in writing or fails to apply for a hearing or fails to attend the hearing, the application shall be dismissed.

If the Application is found to be in order, the Registrar accepts the Application and publishes it in the ensuing GI Journal.

3.6. Correction and Amendment of Application:

The applicant may, anytime before or after acceptance but before registration, may apply in **Form GI -5** with the prescribed fee for correction of any error in or in connection with his Application or any amendment in his Application provided such proposed amendments does not relate to the amendment of the GI or description of Goods or to the definite territory, region or locality, as the case may be, that would not have the substantially altering or substituting the original application.

Form GI -5

Fees: 300/-

An amendment of GI or in the description of goods, or the territory, region or locality that would have the effect of substantially altering or substituting the original application will not be allowed.

3.7. Acceptance

The Registrar may accept the GI Application absolutely or subject to such amendments, modification, conditions or limitations as he thinks fit.

The objections and/or proposal for conditional acceptance are to be communicated to the applicant.

In case of objections to the acceptance of the application or conditional acceptance, the grounds of objection or for refusal or conditional acceptance and the materials used by him arriving at the decision shall be recorded.

3.8. Advertisement in GI Journal:

Sec 13: Advertisement of application

Rule 38: Manner of advertisement

The Registrar of GI publishes all the GI Applications and authorised user applications in the Official GI Journal. The GI Journal is being published and is made available to the Public ordinarily in the first week of every month, through the Official Website. CD-ROMs of each Journal can be obtained from the GI Registry on payment of Rs. 250.

GI Application is published with the following details:

(A) Name of Geographical Indication alongwith Logo

(B) GI Application Number:

(C) Name of the Applicant :

(B) Address of the Applicant :

(C) List of association of persons/
Producers / organization/ authority :

(D) Type of Goods & Class :

(E) Statement of Case

Furthermore proceedings are explained in short along with the respective Forms in next Chapter '**Form-Fees-Timeline and Proceedings**'.

Next chapter is very crucial and most of the questions are anticipated from that content.

FOUR

FORMS -FEES-TIMELINE

This book is primarily meant for Trade Mark Agent aspirant to cover the important notes respect to Geographical Indication.

For getting done in minimum period of time, I will recommend you to start this chapter in most productive hours initially and then just chant it whenever, you get time.

There are 10 Forms and 3 petitions having total 38 entries that you need to take care.

Let me explain, the entries in brief.

Say for example, there is form GI-1 for application for registration of GI, but purposes of Entry 1-A, 1-B, 1-C, and 1-D are different, as stated in Q1. Similarly, different entries have different purposes, as stated at respective tables.

One relief is there while recalling Forms and Fees for GI, only one Fees structure, no complication of remembering different fees for online or type of applicants.

This Chapter is very much important, you are expected to know this. Be ready with this chapter it contains answer of predictable questions respect to GI.

I hope you are recalling there are Two Register of GI

Part A: For entry of GI registration

Part B: For entry of Registration of Authorised User

Let's start.....

4.1. Forms and Fees

Q1. *When to File Form GI-1?*

A. When you are required to file application for the registration of GI as per sec 11 and rule 23 and rule 84.

All the requisite about the application form and content of the documents are discussed in Chapter -'Procedure for GI Registration'.

Form GI-1

Entry No	Purpose	Sec/Rule	Fees (INR)
1-A	On application for the registration of a geographical indication for goods included in one class	[Section 11(1), rule 23(2)].	5000/-
1-B	On application for the registration of a geographical indication for goods included in one class from a convention country	[Section 11(1), 84(1), rule 23(3)	5000/-
1-C	On a single application for the registration of a geographical indication for goods in different classes	[Section 11(3) rule 23(5)].	5000/- Each class
1-D	On a single application for the registration of a geographical indication for goods in different classes from a convention country.	[Section 11(3), 84(1), rule 23(4)].	5000/- Each class

ᐅᐅᐅ

Q2. *When to File Form GI-2?*

A. Form GI-2 is used for filing notice of opposition and counterstatement and extension respect to filing notice of opposition.

Notice of opposition-*[Sec 14]*:

Who?: Any Person

When?: within **three months** from date of advertisement of a Geographical Indication in the Geographical Indications Journal.

Extension?: Maximum of further **one month.**

Requirements of Notice of opposition:

- a statement of the grounds upon which the opponents objects to the registration of the geographical indication. [Rule 41]
- Fees + Form GI-2[Entry No 2-A]
- The notice of opposition shall be verified by the opponent. [Rule 42]

Counterstatement-*[Rule 43]*:

Who?: Applicant whose application received notice of opposition.

When?: Within two months from the receipt of notice of opposition.

Extension: Not possible

Requirements of Counterstatement.

- Counter Statement shall set out what facts, if any, alleged in the notice of opposition, are admitted by the applicant.
- Fees + Form GI-2 [Entry No 2-B]
- The counterstatement shall be verified.

Form GI-2

Entry No	Purpose	Sec/Rule	Fees
2-A	On a notice of opposition to the registration of a geographical indication under section 14(1)	Section 14(1)	1000/- Each class
	or an opposition to an authorised user Section 17(3)(e).	Section 17(3)(e)	
2-B	On a counter-statement in answer to a notice of opposition under section 14(2) or 17(3)(e)	section 14(2) or 17(3)(e)	1000/-
	for each application opposed and in answer to an application under section 27 in respect of each geographical indication or in answer to a notice of opposition under section 29.	section 27 section 29	
2-C	On application for extension of time for filing notice of opposition.	[Section 14(1), 17(3)(e), 29(2), rule 41(5)]	300/-

ᐅᐅᐅ

Q3. *When to File Form GI-3?*

A. Form GI-3 is used for application for registration of authorised user and its renewal.

Who?: Any person claiming to be producer of the goods for which a geographical indication has been registered under sec 16 of the GI Act, then such person may apply for the registration as Authorised User.

Renewal: The registration of Authorised User is also for 10 years or expires with the term of Gi Registration whichever is earlier and required to renew before expiry period. [Sec 18(2)]

Form GI-3

Entry No	Purpose	Sec/Rule	Fees
3-A	On application for the registration of an authorised user of a registered geographical indication under	section 17, Rule 56(1)	10/-
3-B	For renewal of an authorised user	Sec18(2), rule 60(1)	10/-

Q4. When to File Form GI-4?

A. Form GI-4 is used for renewal of GI registration or for renewal with surcharge and for restoration of GI registration & registration of authorised user.

Duration for which GI registration is Valid: Ten years

When you can start renewal process?: From Six Months before the date of Expiry.

Renewal with surcharge: Within six months from date of expiry of Registration.

Restoration of GI: After Six months and within one year from the expiration of the last registration. [Rule 63]

Form GI-4

Entry No	Purpose	Sec/Rule	Fees
4-A	For renewal under section 18(1) of the registration of a geographical indication at the expiration of the last registration.	Rule 60(1)	3000/-
4-B	On application under section 18(5) for restoration of geographical indication or an authorised user removed from the Register.	Sec 18 (5) rule 63	1000/- + Applicable renewal fees
4-C	On application for renewal under proviso to section 18(4) Proviso to rule 62 within six months from the expiration of last registration of geographical indication.	section 18(4) rule 62	3500/-

ᐳᐳᐳ

Q5. *When to File Form GI-5?*

A. Form GI-5 is required to file for following purpose;

- when it is required to correct the address of Principal Place of business, error in name or need to correct description of
- Application for Rectification of the register In Part B i.e for rectification of authorised user registration.
- Application for division of application.
- For search in the GI register respect to existing registration in said class/ goods.

Form GI-5

Entry No	Purpose	Sec/Rule	Fees
5-A	On request for alteration of the address of the principal place of business or of residence in India or of the address in the home country abroad in the Register of Geographical Indications are authorised user	Section 28 Rule 69	300/-
5-B	On request to enter change in name or description of proprietor of geographical indication upon the Register.		300/-
5-C	On request for correction of any error in the name , address or description of the registered proprietor or the authorised user of a geographical indication.	(Section 28(a)).	300/-
5-D	On application for the rectification of the register in Part B for the removal of an authorised user.	Section 27 Rule 65	1000/-
5-E	On division of goods in a class or on division of an application made for registration of a geographical indication in different classes under proviso to Section 15, rule 23(7).	Section 15 rule 23(7)	1000/-
5-F	For a search under rule 22 in respect of one class.	Rule 22	500/-

ᕗᕗᕗ

Q6. *When to File Form GI-6?*

A. Form GI-6 is required to file for following purposes;

- rectification of the register/ cancelling /varying entry/expunge the registration of GI or Authorised User.
- for intervention of the rectification proceedings by third party.

Rectification-[Sec 27]

Who?: Any person aggrieved

Where?: High Court / Registrar

Grounds: Any contravention /failure to observe the condition entered on the Register

When?: Any time After Registration

Entry No	Purpose	Sec/Rule	Fees
6-A	On application under section 27 for rectification of the register or removal of a geographical indication or expunge or vary the Statement of the Case under rule 32(1) recorded in the Register or an authorised user from the register,. Rule 65		1000/-
6-B	On application for leave to intervene in proceedings relating to the rectification of the Register or for the removal of a geographical indication or an authorised user from the Register.	Rule 67 Rule 80(4).	500/-

ᐅᐅᐅ

Q7. *When to File Form GI-7?*

A. Form GI-7 is for the following purposes

- request for obtaining Certificate of the Registrar.
- for furnishing affidavit in support of statement of case.
- for advertisement of particulars of GI.
- for requesting duplicate copy of certificate.
- Application for review of the decision

Review of Decision -[Sec 60(c); Rule 97]

When?: Within one month from the date of decision

Extension: Maximum extension of one month is possible

Requirements: An application and a statement setting forth the ground on which review is sought.

Form GI-7

Entry No	Purpose	Sec/Rule	Fees
7-A	On request for certificate of Registrar [other than a certificate under Section 69 or 78(1)].	Rule 96	300/-
7-B	Affidavit in support of statement of case or other documents required under the Act or rules.		Nill
7-C	On request for entry in the Register and advertisement of a note of certificate of validity of the Appellate Board.	Rule 99	200/-
7-D	On application for review of Registrar's decision.		500/-
7-E	On request to registrar for particulars of advertisement of a geographical indication		100/-
7-F	On request to Registrar for a duplicate or further copy of certificate		200/-

ÞÞÞ

Q8. When to File Form GI-8?

A. The Form GI -8 is related to all the formalities respect to registration, correction, renewal and restoration of name in the register of Geographical Indication Agent.

Time to mind:

- Application for continuance as GI Agent to be made every year, on or before 1st April.
- Application for restoration of name in the Register of GI agent is to be made within six months.

Form GI-8

Entry No	Purpose	Sec/Rule	Fees
8-A	Application for registration of a geographical indications agent.	Rule 107	1000/-
8-B	On request for issuance of certificate as geographical indications agent.	Rule 109.	1000/-
8-C	For continuance of the name of a person in the Register of Geographical Indication Agent under rule 110; - For every year (excluding the first year) to be paid on 1st April in each year. - For the first year to be paid along with the fee for registration, in the case of a person registered at any time between the 1st April, and 30th September. N.B: A year for this purpose will commence on the 1st day of April and end on the 31st day of March following.		1000/-
8-D	On application for restoration of the name of a person to the Register of Geographical Indications	rule 113	1000/-+ continuous fees

ᐳᐳᐳ

Q9. When to File Form GI-9?

A. Form GI-9 is used for the following purposes;

- Application for additional protection of Certain goods.
- Alteration of Registered GI
- Requesting Extension during furnishing evidences and in all other proceedings, where provision of extension is provided but form is not prescribed.

Form GI-9

Entry No	Purpose	Sec/Rule	Fees
9-A	On application to Registrar for additional protection to certain goods.	Section 22(2) rule 77(1).	25000/-
9-B	On application for leave to add or alter a registered geographical indication [except where the application is made by an or of a public authority or in consequence of a statutory requirement.	Section 29	300/-
9-C	On application for extension of time not being a time expressly provided in the Act or prescribed in the rules..	Rule 83	300/-

ᗐᗐᗐ

Q10. When to File Form GI-10?

A. Form GI-10 is used for the following purposes;

- For striking out the goods from the register
- Furnishing power of authorisation

Form GI-10

Entry No	Purpose	Sec/Rule	Fees
10-A	On application for cancellation of an entry in the Register or to strike out goods.	(Section 28(c) or (d)).	300/-
10-B	Form of authorisation of agent in a matter or proceedings under the Act.	Section 76, Rule 20	Nill

ᏤᏤᏤ

Petitions

There are certain purposes such as obtaining interlocutory matter from the Registrar in a contested proceeding or inspection of documents; for which no Forms are suggested, instead petitions need to file.

One more petition for obtaining photocopy of document is also suggested in GI rule, however, now GI register is available on the official website of CGPDTM 'www.ipindia.gov.in'.

Entry No	Purpose	Sec/Rule	Fees
11	On petition (not otherwise charged) for obtaining the Registrar's order on any interlocutory matter in a contested proceeding.		500/-
12	For inspecting the document mentioned in Section 78(1)-	Section 78(1)	
	a) relating to any particular geographical indication or authorised user thereof for every hour or part thereof;		100/-
	b) computer search (when made available) for every 15 minutes;		100/-
	c) Search of index mentioned in section 78 for every hour or part thereof		100/-
13	For copying of documents (photocopy or typed) for every page or part thereof in excess of one page		10/-

Forms to be used by the Registrar

Form O-1 to O-5 are used by the Registrar for communication from GI Registry.

Form	Purpose	Sec/Rule
O-1	Notice of non-completion of registration	Section16(3)
O-2	Certificate of registration of geographical indication	Rule 55(1)
O-3	Notice of expiration of last registration.	Rule 61
O-4	Certificate of registration of a person as a geographical Indication	Rule 102
O-5	Notice of expiration of last registration of an authorised user	Rule 55(1)

ᗺᗺᗺ

Question Bank on Timeline

Q11. Time within which applicant need to remedy any deficiencies after 'Issuance of Formality Check Report under Rule 31 to remedy the deficiencies in the application for Registration of G.I.' is ...

A. Within One month failuer to do results into 'treated as abandoned'.

Q12. Compliance of the notice under rule 31 to remedy the deficiencies in the application for Registration of G.I

A. Within one *month* from the date of Receipt of the Notice

Q13. Finalization of examination of application by the Consultative Group

Within three *months* from the date of constitution of the consultative group

Q14. Advertisement

Within three *months* of the acceptance of the application

Q15. Registration

Average time taken Twelve *months* from the date of Receipt of Application

Q16. Notice of opposition

Within three *months* or further period not exceeding one *month* in the aggregate from the date when the Journal was made available to the public

Q17. Forwarding of the copy of notice of opposition to the applicant

Within two *months* of the receipt of the notice by the Registrar

Q18. Filing of counter statement

Within two *months* from the receipt of the applicant of the copy of the notice of opposition from the Registrar

Q19. Serving of the counter statement on Opponent

Within two *months* from the date of receipt of the counter statement by the Registrar

Q20. Evidence in support of opposition by the opponent

A. Within two *months* from the date of serving of the copy of the counter statement or within such further period not exceeding *one month* in the aggregate thereafter as the Registrar may on request allow

Q21. Filing of Evidence in reply by opponent

A. With in *one month* from the receipt by the opponent of the copies of the applicant"s affidavits or within such further period not exceeding *one month* thereafter as the Registrar may on request allow

Q22. Notice for Hearing

A. Within *3 months* of completion of the evidence

Q23. Transmission of application and statement for the rectification.

A. Within two *months* of receipt of the application by the Registrar

Q24. Filing of Counter-Statement by Registered Proprietors

A. Within two *months* or within further period not exceeding two *months* in the aggregate from the receipt of the copy of the application for rectification by Registered Proprietor

Q25. Serving of the counter statement on the applicant

A. Within one *month* from the date of receipt of the counter statement by the Registrar

Q26. Evidence in support of Rectification by the Applicant

A. Within two *months* from the date of serving of the copy of the counter statement or within such further period not exceeding one *month* in the aggregate thereafter as the Registrar may on request allow

Q27. Evidence in support of Registered G.I. by the Registered Proprietor

A. Within two *months* or within such further period not exceeding one *month* thereafter in aggregate as the Registrar may on request allow, on the receipt by the Registered Proprietor of the copies of affidavits in support of rectification or of the intimation that the applicant doesn"t desire to adduce any evidence.

Q28. Filing of Evidence in reply by Applicant

A. With in *one month* from the receipt by the applicant of the copies of the Registered Proprietor"s affidavits or within such further period not exceeding *one month* thereafter as the Registrar may on request allow

Q29. Notice for Hearing

A. Within *3 months* of completion of the evidence

Q30. Appeal to the HC

A. Within *3 months* from the date on which the order or decision sought to be appealed against is communicated to such person preferring the appeal.

This chapter is very crucial, if you work on this chapter hard you can solve majority of the questions asked based on the conepts of Geographical Indication Act and Rule.

Next chapter deals with -Classes.

FIVE

CLASSES

It is mandatory to apply in relevamt class to apply for GI tag for your particular goods.

As per Sec 8 (2) Registration to be in respect of particular good

"The Registrar shall classify the goods under in accordance with the international Classification of goods for the purpose of the registration of Geographical Indication."

As per Rule 21. Classification of goods:

"For the purposes of the registration of a geographical indication or as an authorised user, goods shall be classified in the manner specified in the Fourth Schedule." [Rule 21(1)]

"The goods mentioned in the Fourth Schedule only provide a means by which the general content of numbered international classes can be quickly identified. They correspond to the major content of each class and are not intended to be exhaustive in accordance with the International Classification of Goods. For determining the classification of particular goods and for full disclosure of the content of international classification, reference may be made to the alphabetical index of goods if any, published by the Registrar under sub-section (3) of section 8 or the current edition of International Classification of Goods for the purpose of registration of trade marks published by the World Intellectual Property Organisation or any subsequent edition as may be available." [Rule 21(2)]

"Where goods of more than one class are set out in an application for which only one application fee has been paid, the Registrar shall require the applicant to amend the application in order to restrict the goods to a single class."[Rule 21 (3)]

That means Nice classification available for goods only are valid for determining class of the goods under application.

following is the list of classes for the respective goods obtained form the www.ipindia.gov.in.

Additionally, the GI register is squeezed for the application and registration. Total 1379 applications are mentioned in that. Following list of class is provided with the relevant GI application, wherever, possible.

Most of the GI application for class 20, 23, 24, 24, 26, 27, 28, 30, 31.

Then GI application/Registration is observed class 2, 3, 4, 6, 8, 12, 14, 15, 16, 18, 19, 21, 29, 33, 34.

Some of foreign application/Registration are observed in Class 32: that include Scotch Whisky and Peruvian Pisco.

THE FOURTH SCHEDULE

Classification of goods– Name of the classes

(Parts of an article or apparatus are, in general, classified with the actual article or apparatus, except where such parts constitute articles included in other classes).

Class 1.

Chemical used in industry, science, photography, agriculture, horticulture and forestry; unprocessed artificial resins, unprocessed plastics; manures; fire extinguishing compositions; tempering and soldering preparations; chemical substances for preserving foodstuffs; tanning substances; adhesive used in industry.

Class 2.

Paints, varnishes, lacquers; preservatives against rust and against deterioration of wood; colorants; mordents; raw natural resins; metals in foil and powder form for painters;decorators; printers and artists

Eg. GI Registration No.1159
Geographical Indication: Kongarapattu Indigo Dye
Applicant:Cirana Earth Foundation
Goods:Natural Goods
Geographical Area:

Other examples are GI appl No 1242 for Kusumi Lac.

Class 3.

Bleaching preparations and other substances for laundry use; cleaning; polishing; scouring and abrasive preparations; soaps; perfumery, essential oils, cosmetics, hair lotions, dentifrices

Eg. GI Registration No. 13
Geographical Indication: Mysore Agarbathi
Applicant: All India Agarbathi Manufacturers Association
Goods: Manufactured
Geographical Area: Karnataka

Class 4.

Industrial oils and greases; lubricants; dust absorbing, wetting and binding compositions; fuels(including motor spirit) and illuminants; candles, wicks.

Eg. GI Registration Appl No.38
Geographical Indication:Jamnagar Petrol
Applicant: Reliance Industries Limited
Goods:Natural
Geographical Area: Gujarat

Class 5.

Pharmaceutical, veterinary and sanitary preparations; dietetic substances adapted for medical use, food for babies; plasters, materials for dressings; materials for stopping teeth, dental wax; disinfectants; preparation for destroying vermin; fungicides, herbicides

Class 6.

Common metals and their alloys; metal building materials; transportable buildings of metal; materials of metal for railway tracks; non-electric cables and wires of common metal; ironmongery, small items of metal hardware; pipes and tubes of metal; safes; goods of common metal not included in other classes; ores.

Eg. GI Registration Appl No. 53

Geographical Indication:Silver Filigree of Karimnagar
Applicant:Karimnagar Silver Filigree Handicrafts Mutually Aided Co-Operative Welfare Society Limited
Goods:Handicraft
Geographical Area:Telangana

Class 7.

Machines and machine tools; motors and engines (except for land vehicles); machine coupling and transmission components (except for land vehicles); agricultural implements other than hand-operated; incubators for eggs

Class 8.

Hand tools and implements (hand-operated); cutlery; side arms; razors
Eg. GI Registration Appl No. 53
Geographical Indication:Silver Filigree of Karimnagar
Applicant:Karimnagar Silver Filigree Handicrafts Mutually Aided Co-Operative Welfare Society Limited
Goods:Handicraft
Geographical Area:Telangana

Class 9.

Scientific, nautical, surveying, electric, photographic, cinematographic, optical, weighing, measuring, signalling, checking (supervision), life saving and teaching apparatus and instruments; apparatus for recording, transmission or reproduction of sound or images; magnetic data carriers, recording discs; automatic vending machines and mechanisms for coin-operated apparatus; cash registers, calculating machines, data processing equipment and computers; fire extinguishing apparatus

Class 10.

Surgical, medical, dental and veterinary apparatus and instruments, artificial limbs, eyes and teeth; orthopaedic articles; suture materials

Class 11.

Apparatus for lighting, heating, steam generating, cooking, refrigerating, drying ventilating, water supply and sanitary purposes

Class 12.

Vehicles; apparatus for locomotion by land, air or water
   Eg. GI Registration App No.12
   Geographical Indication:Kashmir Houseboat
   Applicant:Department of Handicrafts and Handloom Kashmir
   Goods:Handi Crafts
   Geographical Area: -

Class 13.

Firearms; ammunition and projectiles; explosives; fire works

Class 14.

Precious metals and their alloys and goods in precious metals or coated therewith, not included in other classes; jewellery, precious stones; horological and other chronometric instruments
   Eg. GI Registration No. 6
   Geographical Indication:Payyannur Pavithra Ring
   Applicant:Payyannur pavithra Ring Artisans &Development Society,
   Goods:Handicraft
   Geographical Area:Kerala

Class 15.

Musical instruments
   Eg. GI Registration Appl No.-59
   Geographical Indication: Maddalam of Palakkad
   Applicant:Development Commissioner (Handicrafts)
   Goods:Handicraft
   Geographical Area:Kerala

Class 16.

Paper, cardboard and goods made from these materials, not included in other classes; printed matter; bookbinding material; photographs; stationery; adhesives for stationery or household purposes; artists'materials; paint brushes; typewriters and office requisites (except furniture); instructional and teaching material (except apparatus); plastic materials for packaging (not included in other classes); playing cards; printers' type; printing blocks

Eg. GI Registration Appl No-32
Geographical Indication: Mysore Traditional Paintings
Applicant: Karnataka State Handicrafts Development Corporation Limited
Goods:Handicraft
Geographical Area: Karnataka

Class 17.

Rubber, gutta percha, gum, asbestos, mica and goods made from these materials and not included in other classes; plastics in extruded form for use in manufacture; packing, stopping and insulating materials; flexible pipes, not of metal

Class 18.

Leather and imitations of leather, and goods made of these materials and not included in other classes; animal skins, hides, trunks and travelling bags; umbrellas, parasols and walking sticks; whips, harness and saddlery

Eg. GI Registration Appl No. 53
Geographical Indication:Silver Filigree of Karimnagar
Applicant:Karimnagar Silver Filigree Handicrafts Mutually Aided Co-Operative Welfare Society Limited
Goods:Handicraft
Geographical Area:Telangana

Class 19.

Building materials, (non-metallic), non-metallic rigid pipes for building; asphalt, pitch and bitumen; non-metallic transportable buildings; monuments, not of metal.

Eg. GI Registration Appl No.52
Geographical Indication:Nakshi Kantha
Applicant:KAARU – KUL FOUNDATION,
Goods:Handicraft
Geographical Area:West Bengal

Class 20.

Furniture, mirrors, picture frames; goods(not included in other classes) of wood, cork, reed, cane, wicker, horn, bone, ivory, whalebone, shell, amber, mother- of-pearl, meerschaum and substitutes for all these materials, or of plastics.

Eg. GI Registration No. 3:
Geographical Indication: Aranmula Kannadi (Aranmula Metal Mirror)
Applicant: Viswabrahmana Aranmula Kannadi Nirman Society
Goods: Handicraft
Geographical Area: Kerala

Class 21.

Household or kitchen utensils and containers(not of precious metal or coated therewith); combs and sponges; brushes(except paints brushes); brush making materials; articles for cleaning purposes; steelwool; unworked or semi-worked glass (except glass used in building); glassware, porcelain and earthenware not included in other classes

Eg. GI Registration Appl No.20
Geographical Indication:Bidriware
Applicant:Karnataka State Handicrafts Development Corporation Limited
Goods:Handicraft
Geographical Area:Karnataka

Class 22.

Ropes, string, nets, tents, awnings, tarpaulins, sails, sacks and bags (not included in other classes) padding and stuffing materials(except of rubber or plastics); raw fibrous textile materials

Eg. GI Registration App No.1353

Geographical Indication: Yak Wool Fabric & Pu Chuppa (Jacket)

Applicant:1. Arunachal Pradesh Yak Herders and Products Development Cooperative Society and

2. ICAR – National Research Centre on Yak (ICAR - NRC) of Arunachal Pradesh

Goods: Handi Crafts

Geographical Area:-(Application is in process)

Class 23.

Yarns and threads, for textile use

Eg. GI Registration No-11

Geographical Indication: Mysore Silk

Applicant: Karnataka Silk Industries Corporation Limited

Goods: Handicraft

Geographical Area: Karnataka

[This GI is also registered undwer class 24 and class 25]

Class 24.

Textiles and textile goods, not included in other classes; bed and table covers.

Eg. GI Registration Appl No-9

Geographical Indication: Solapur Terry Towel

Applicant: Textile Development Foundation

Goods: Handicraft

Geographical Area: Maharashtra

Class 25.

Clothing, footwear, headgear

Eg. GI Registration App No. 51

Geographical Indication:Kani Shawl

Applicant:TAHAFUZ

Goods:Handicraft

Geographical Area:Jammu & Kashmir

Class 26.

Lace and embroidery, ribbons and braid; buttons, hooks and eyes, pins and needles; artificial flowers

Eg. GI Registration No.27
Geographical Indication:Phulkari
Applicant:Punjab Small Industries & Export Corporation Ltd.
Goods:Embroidery
Geographical Area: India (Punjab, Haryana & Rajasthan)

Class 27.

Carpets, rugs, mats and matting, linoleum and other materials for covering existing floors; wall hangings(non-textile)

Eg. GI Registration Appl No.-54
Geographical Indication:Alleppey Coir
Applicant:Coir Board
Goods:Handicraft
Geographical Area:Kerala

Class 28.

Games and playthings, gymnastic and sporting articles not included in other classes; decorations for Christmas trees

Eg. GI Registration Appl No. 53
Geographical Indication:Silver Filigree of Karimnagar
Applicant:Karimnagar Silver Filigree Handicrafts Mutually Aided Co-Operative Welfare Society Limited
Goods:Handicraft
Geographical Area:Telangana
Eg. GI Registration Appl No. 68
Geographical Indication:Kathputlis of Rajasthan
Applicant:Development Commissioner (Handicrafts)
Goods:Handicraft
Geographical Area:Rajasthan

Class 29.

Meat, fish, poultry and game; meat extracts; preserved, dried and cooked fruits and vegetables; jellies, jams, fruit sauces; eggs, milk and milk products; edible oils and fats

Eg. GI Registration Appl No. 80
Geographical Indication:Dharwad Pedha
Applicant:Thakur's Dharwad Pedha Manufacturers' Welfare Trust
Goods:Food Stuffs
Geographical Area:Karnataka

Class 30.

Coffee, tea, cocoa, sugar, rice, tapioca, sago, artificial coffee; flour and preparations made from cereals, bread, pastry and confectionery, ices; honey, treacle; yeast, baking powder; salt, mustard; vinegar, sauces, (condiments); spices; ice

Eg. GI Registration No. 49
Geographical Indication:Malabar Pepper
Applicant:Spices Board, (A Commodity Board, Under The Ministry of Commerce and Industry)
Goods: Agriculture
Geographical Area:India (Kerala, Karnataka & Tamilnadu)

Class 31.

Agricultural, horticultural and forestry products and grains not included in other classes; live animals; fresh fruits and vegetables; seeds, natural plants and flowers; foodstuffs for animals, malt

Eg. GI Registration No. 50
Geographical Indication:Allahabad Surkha Guava
Applicant:Allahabad Surkha
Goods: Agriculture
Geographical Area:Uttar Pradesh

Class 32.

Beers, mineral and aerated waters, and other non-alcoholic drinks; fruit drinks and fruit juices; syrups and other preparations for making beverages

Eg. GI Registration Appl No.1360

Geographical Indication:Tiptur Coconut and Coconut Products

Applicant:1.Tiptur Farmer Producer Company Ltd (TFPC) and 2.Agricultural Produce Market Committee (APMC) Tiptur

Goods:Agriculture

Geographical Area:[Application is in process]

Class 33.

Alcoholic beverages(except beers)

Eg. GI Registration No.43

Geographical Indication:Peruvian Pisco

Applicant:Embassy of Peru

Goods:Manufactured

Geographical Area:Peru

Class 34.

Tobacco, smokers' articles, matches

Eg. GI Registration No. 20

Geographical Indication:Bidriware

Applicant:Karnataka State Handicrafts Development Corporation Limited

Goods: Handicraft

Geographical Area: Karnataka

This chapter is giving you better isight for classes and the respective examples applied or registered as per GI Register.

Reader can check couple of examples, so that clear idea can be obtained respect to the content of applications and all proceedings.

Next chapter provides- 'Case Studies'

SIX

CASE STUDIES

Case studies plays very important role in any legislation, something is required to exercise first time for that case and that case becomes the mile stone in that field and refered numerous time to prove your point or for imparting instructions to the pupiles.

Case 1: First Registered Geographical Indication in India

[Following details are obtained from the 'Register Of Geographical Indication' as published on the website of 'www.ipindia.gov.in' for the academic purpose and for imparting instruction to the pupiles only and not to be used for any legislative dispute.]

First ever GI Application NO -1 is of Darjeeling Tea (word); filled in the Indian Jurisdiction.

GI Application No-2 and its registration is also owned by Darjeeling Tea (Logo)

Wherein, said GI application was made with the following details.

Applicant: TEA BOARD, a statutory authority of the Government of India established in 1953 under the tea Act, 1953 for the purpose of Controlling Indian Tea Industry.

Address: 14 B.T.M Sarani (Brabourne Road), PO Box2172, Kolkatta-700001,India.

Geographical Indication: DARJEELING

Goods: Darjeeling Tea

Class: 30

Type of goods: Tea grown in 87 gardens in the district of Darjeeling falling in class 30.

Specification: Tea produced in the said region has the distinctive and naturally occurring organoleptic characteristic of taste, aroma and mouth feel which have won the patronage and recognition of discerning consumers all over the world.

Name of geographical indication and particulars:

Darjeeling Tea. The 87 Garden, the details of which are furnished under the head Geographical Area production and Map located within the Darjeeling District, cultivating, growing/producing Darjeeling Tea.

Due to unique and complex combination of agro-climatic conditions prevailing in the region comprising the said 87 gardens within the district of Darjeeling and the production regulations imposed by the Board, tea produced in the said region has the distinctive and naturally occurring organoleptic characteristics of the taste, aroma and the mouth feel which have won the patronage and recognition of discerning consumers all over the world. Consequently, tea produced in the said region and having the said special characteristic, is and has for long being known to the trade and public in India and abroad as Darjeeling Tea and as such it has acquired substantial domestic and international reputation. Any member of the trade or public in India or abroad ordering Darjeeling tea or seeing tea advertised or offered for sale as Darjeeling will expect the tea so ordered, advertised or offered for sale to be tea cultivated, grown and produced in the aforesaid region of the Darjeeling district and having the aforesaid special characteristics.

Description of the goods: The botanical name of the Darjeeling tea plant is 'camellia sinensis'. It has hardy, multi stemmed, slow growing evergreen shrub which if allowed to, can grow up to 2.5 meters in height. It takes 4-6 years to mature and is known to have economic life of well over 100 years with good care. It is able to withstand severe winters, extended droughts and the high altitudes of Darjeeling. The yields are much lower than non-Darjeeling tea is a result of combination of plant genes, soil chemistry, elevations, temperature and rainfall unique to the Darjeeling hills. A set of agricultural practice has been developed to sustain growth of shoots, while maintaining bush heights suitable for manual plucking. Plucking begins in March and closes by late November. A Darjeeling tea bush yields only 100 gms of made tea in a year. Each kilogram of fine tea consist of more than 20,000 individual hand picked shoots. This gives an idea of the extent of human effort involved in its production.

Geographical area of production and Map shown in actual application

List of 87 Gardens:

1. Allobari; 2. Ambiok (Hilton); 3. Arya; 4. Avongrove; 5.Ambootia; 6. Badamtam; 7. Barnesbeg; 8. Bannockburn; 9. Balasun; 10. Chongtong; 11. Chamong; 12. Castleton; 13. Dhajea; 14. Dooteriah; 15. Dilarm; 16. Edenvale; 17. Ging; 18. Gielle, 19. Glenburn; 20. Gopaldhara. 21. Goomtee; 22. Giddapahar; 23. Gyabaree & Millikthong; 24. Happy Valley; 25. Jogmaya; 26. Jungpana (Jungpana upper); 27. Kalej Valley; 28. Kumai (Snowview); 29. Lingia; 30. Liza Hill; 31. Longview (Highland); 32. Lopchu; 33. Margaret; 34.Marybong; 35. Mim ; 36. Mission Hill ; 37.Moondakotee; 38. Mohan Majhua;39. Makaibari ;40. Mullotar; 41. Mahalderm; 42. Monteviot; 43. Nagi; 44. Nagri Farm; 45. North Tukvar; 46. Narbada Majhua; 47. Nurbong; 48. Namring & Namring (upper); 49.Oaks; 50. Okayti; 51. Orange Valley; 52. Pandam; 53. Pashok; 54. Phoobsering; 55. Poobong; 56. Pussimbing (Minzoo); 57. Phuguri; 58. Rangaroon; 59. Ringtong; 60. Risheehat; 61. Rohini; 62. Runglee Rungliot; 63. Rungmook/Cedars; 64. Rungneer; 65. Samabeong; 66. Seimbong (Rongbong); 67. Soom; 68. Singtom; 69. Steinthal; 70. Sungama; 71. Selim Hill; 72. Singbuli; 73. Sivitar; 74. Springside; 75. Soureni; 76. Singell; 77. Sepoydhoorah (Chamling); 78. Seeyok (Spring Valley); 79. Tukvar (Puttabong); 80. Tumsong; 81. Turzum; 82. Tindharia; 83. Thurbo; 84. Tukdah; 85. Teesta Valley; 86. Upper Fagu; 87. Vah Tukvar.

Proof of origin: [Historical Record]

The extract of Gazetteers of the Darjeeling District published by author Jules Dash, Chairman of the public service commission, Bengal published in the year 1947 containing detailed account of Physical description of Darjeeling Area and about the Tea Industry (121 pages).

Method of production:

Detailed method of production was provided.

[Pls refer, GI application No 1 from the website www.ipindia.gov.in]

Uniqueness:

The distinctive, exclusive and rare character of Darjeeling tea is the result of several factors. The tea gardens are situated at elevations from 610 to 2134 meters on steep slope which provide identical natural drainage for the generous rainfall the district receives. Coupled with this, the intermittent cloud and sunshine combine to import the unique character of Darjeeling tea which has the distinctive and naturally occurring organoleptic characteristics of taste, aroma and mouth feel which have won the patronage and recognition of discerning consumers all over the world.

Inspection body:

Following paragraph is providing excerpt of what has been provided in the application .

"The Tea industry has been under the control of the Central Government since 1933." Furthermore, following all the legislations amended over a period of time.

"In pursuance of its statutory under the Tea Act, 1953 and its predecessor statues, the Board has been implementing a certification program for regulation and control of the all teas administered by it including Darjeeling tea."

"At the production level, all the 87 gardens producing Darjeeling Tea are registered with the board and are required to seek prior approval of the Board for planting tea seeds or extension of area under cultivation. The Board has been regularly monitoring these gardens by making periodical checks and inspections. Every single invoice of tea produced by the aforesaid 87 gardens is sent to the Board, detailing grades quantity and chest number."

"All ware houses are registered with the Board under the Tea warehouse Licensing Order."

"All auction centres and brokers are licensed by the Board including all new auction Centre or Brokers."

" All exporters are registered with the Board under the Tea (Distribution and Export centres)."

"The Board has an arrangement whereby testing or confirmation testing of all Darjeeling tea is carried out by a Panel of Tasters."

According to the applicant all these provisions for inspection bodies is maintaining the distinctive characteristics associated with a particular type of Darjeeling tea.

Other:

Certificate of Registration obtained in India for Darjeeling Logo as certification Mark

Well known dictionaries have defined Darjeeling as a Geographical Region in India Famous for Black

Case 2: GI Application No-2: Darjeeling Tea (Logo)

All applicants and details are nearly same only following difference is there
Geographical Indication:

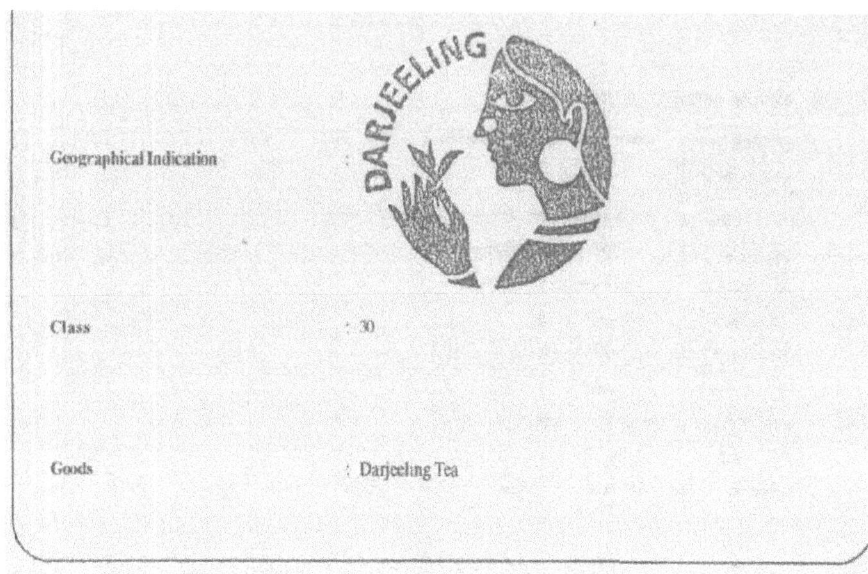

{Above Picture is screenshot from GI register Published on the
www.ipindia.gov.in}

Couple of cases based on the Darjeeling Tea conflicts:

Overall, the 'TEA BOARD' faced more than 15 cases against infringement and misuse of Geographical Indication 'Darjeeling Tea' and logo as shown in case 2.

Tea Board was successful in seeking rejection of trademark application for DARJEELING NOUVEAU in the name of Republic of Tea ("ROT") on the basis of its geographical certification marks for DARJEELING word and logo.

The opposition had been filed by the Tea Board before the Trademark Trial and Appeal Board (TTAB) which has not only upheld Tea Board's opposition but also denied ROT's counterclaim for cancellation of the DARJEELING certification mark on grounds of genericness.

Another case is of 'Darjeeling with a kettle device': The Court of Appeal of Paris on November 22, 2006 quashed the decision of the Court of First Instance rendered in August 2005 wherein the action filed by the Tea Board for dilution of Darjeeling against adoption of the mark "Darjeeling with a kettle device" in respect of classes 16, 35 and 41 by Mr. Dusong.

In its decision, the Court of Appeal, Paris held that Mr. Dusong's mark impairs the geographical indication DARJEELING and is prejudicial to the Tea Board's interests in the same. Accordingly the impugned mark was nullified. Mr. Dusong has been restrained from using the same in any connection whatsoever.

Case 3: Navara Rice

GI application No -17

Applicant for the said application is Navara Rice Farmers Society, Karukamanikalam, Kerala.

Uniqueness: The Navara Rice is the indigenous medicinal plant of Kerala. It has unique medicinal characteristics and hence widely used in Ayurvedic treatments. Navara rice is easily digestrible and hence a light food and has got a unique taste. The short span of about sixty days to mature is unique to Navara rice. The yield of Navara is very poor due to its short duration and susceptibility of the plant to the weather changes. The plant lodges in wind and even in dew during winter season.

The GI got registered in 2007 and applicant imposed condition that 'Only farmers belonging to this society can sell their produce as *Navara rice*'. On another side its not the Kerala only but the Farmers from Tamilnadu also cultivates the said rice crop.

Another point of conflict is this claimant aslso says that *"Nobody has evidence on the historical origin of Navara rice. Besides, you cannot grant GI on seeds, because with migration, seeds also migrate and adapt to local ecology with genetic changes."* and hence more clarity about the legilation is required.

Case 4: Kolhapuri Chappal

GI application No -169

Geographical Origin:

The geographical area of Production of Kolhapuri Chappal covers parts Maharashtra and Karnataka.

The Area of production of Kolhapuri Chappal in Maharashtra comprises of Sholapur, Sangli, Kolhapur and Satara districts.

The Area of production of Kolhapuri Chappal in Karnataka comprises of Dharwad, Belgaum, Bagalkot and Bijapur districts

GI Tag got granted in 2018 for two states and 8 district in order to protect the GI from getting copiied illegaly by any other inlcuding foreign imitation threat.

Case 5: Tirupathi Laddu

GI Application No-121

Applicant: Tirumala Tirupati Devasthanam

GI got registered in 2009 for class 30.

Registration of this GI rasied many questions and actual practice of IP jurisprudence is somwhere got hindered accordin to the opinion of many experts.

Tirupathi Laddu offered as *prasadam* to the devotees after they worship Lord Venkateshwara, the presiding deity at Sri Vari Temple in Tirupathi, Andhra Pradesh.

Invalidation of GI Registration is raised based on following points:

How the GI was granted to a single producer?

Proof of distinctiveness is also under question

And its very generic nature of name and practice to offer laddu as prasadam.

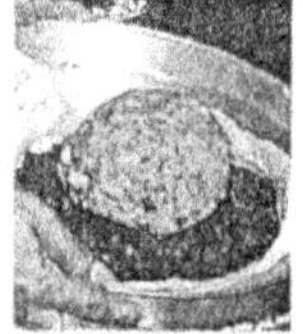

STATES   Hindu BusinessLine 26/10/10   www.businessline.in/states   21

Registry moved for removal of GI tag for 'Tirupati Laddu'

Vinson Kurian

Thiruvananthapuram, Oct 25

An application has been registered with the Geographical Indications (GI) Registry seeking removal of the entry pertaining to 'Tirupati Laddu' GI.

The 'rectification application' has been moved by Mr R S Praveen Raj, an IPR expert and a scientist, with the National Institute for Interdisciplinary Sciences and Technology (NIIST) here.

HIGH COURT ORDER

This follows a Madras High Court order directing a public interest writ petitioner to approach the Intellectual Property Appellate Board (IPAB) or the GI Registry for relief in the matter.

Mr Praveen Raj said he had earlier petitioned the IPAB seeking a 'suo motu' action in the matter. However, the IPAB had replied in the negative saying it lacked 'suo motu' powers.

He had also flagged concerns about applicability of public interest under Section 27 of Geographical Indication of Goods (Registration & Protection) Act, 1999, and Rule 65 of the Geographical Indication of Goods (Registration & Protection) Rules, 2002.

'PERSON AGGRIEVED'

Absence of any response from IPAB in this regard was indicative of suggesting the petitioner to avail the advantage of 'person aggrieved' or

Laddu prasadam

'person interested' to represent public interest, Mr Raj said.

He reserved the option to approach IPAB was being reserved for future, as its jurisdiction could be evoked, if required, in the form of appeal against the order of the Registrar.

Explaining the grounds on which he disagreed with the GI tag, he said GIs are supposed to refer to collective community rights protecting a group of producers but 'Tirupati laddu' fails to conform to this category.

IPR LIMITATIONS

Intellectual Property Rights (IPRs) with reasonable restrictions are allowed only because it is essential for industrial growth of the country. But no industrial purpose is served by the grant of 'goods' status to a temple offering.

'Tirupati laddu' could not be classified either as an 'agricultural' or 'natural' good or even a handicraft, leaving an option to schedule it under 'industrial good.'

But it is quite hard for devotees to digest the fact about temple offerings being equated with a manufactured good or a commercially significant commodity, Mr Raj said.

WRONG MESSAGE

GI tag also tends to pass off a wrong message to the public that temple 'prasadams' (sacred foods) are skin to 'industrial good.'

Mr Raj also found the GI a serious prejudice to Article 25 and Article 26 of the Constitution since it is dangerous to allow private appropriation (especially in the form of IPR) of religious symbols.

(Above screenshot is taken from GI Register)

The GI registration is valid upto 2028 as per the GI register.

(Disclaimer : These all examples are for academic purpose and author don't have any personal interest in any case study.)

In book and in particular Chapter -Five: Classes, numerous GI application Numbers are provided, which can be easily accessed form the website www.ipindia.gov.in

Next chapter provides 'Solution for GI based question asked in TAE-2025 & Mini Question Bank'.

SEVEN

TAE-2025 QUESTIONS: PAPER-I-GI

This chapter provides solved TAE-2025 questions based on GI matter only.

The Part B of the chapter provides Mini Question Bank for GI based questions only.

Some sample questions for both paper I and Paper II.

Part A: TAE-2025 Questions-Paper -I-GI

7.1. TAE-2025 Questions-Paper -I

Following questions are taken from Set Code -A of Paper -I of TAE 2025.

1. Q. 36. The term 'Geographical Indications' could be used for:

   a) Agricultural Goods
   b) Natural Goods
   c) Manufactured Goods
   d) All the above

1. Q. 37. Which was the first Indian goods to get the geographical indication tag?

   a) Aranmula Kannadi
   b) Madhubani Paintings

c) Katarni Rice
d) Darjeeling Tea

3. Q. 38. Which of the following is the benefit of getting GI Tag?

    i. It helps consumers to get quality goods of desired traits.
    ii. Legal protection to the goods
    iii. Promotes the economic prosperity of the producers of GI tagged goods
    Choose the correct answer from the options given below:
    a) Only i and ii
    b) Only i and iii
    c) Only ii
    d) All i, ii and iii

4. Q. 5 Match the following Geographical Indications with concerned GI tags:

    Column – I : Column II
    A. Coimbatore i. Embroidery
    B. Kutch ii. Orange
    C. Coorg iii. Tea
    D. Kangra iv. Wet Grinder
    Choose the correct answer from the options given below:
    a) A:i, B:ii, C:iv, D:iii
    b) A:iv, B:ii, C:iii, D:i
    c) A:iii, B:i, C:ii, D:iv
    d) A:iv, B:i, C:ii, D:iii

5. Q. 6 The geographical indication tag to a product named Tamenglong Orange is associated with which State in India?

    a) Nagaland
    b) Manipur
    c) Rajasthan
    d) Uttar Pradesh

6. Q. 67. Which of the following statements is TRUE about the Geographical Indications of Goods (Registration and Protection) Act, 1999?

a) The GI Act protects only agricultural goods

b) The GI tag can be obtained for both goods and services

c) The GI Act provides protection against unauthorized use of the GI

d) The GI Act is applicable only to goods manufactured in India

7. Q. 68. What is a homonymous geographical indication?

a) A geographical indication that is unique to one region

b) A geographical indications that share the same name, but designate different geographical regions

c) A geographical indication that is not recognized legally

d) A geographical indication that is only applicable to agricultural goods

8. Q. 69. What is currently the prescribed fee for making an application for an authorized user of a Geographical Indication in India?

a)   ₹100

b)   ₹500

c)   ₹10

d)   ₹1000

9. Q. 88. In which scenario can a trade mark containing a geographical origin be registered?

a) If it has acquired a distinctive character as a result of the use made of it

b) If it is already registered internationally

c) If it is commonly used in trade

d) If it is the name of a well-known region

10. Q. 92. What does Section 25 of Geographical Indications of Goods (Registration and Protection) Act, 1999 prohibit regarding geographical indications?

a) Registration of geographical indications as a trade mark

b) Use of the geographical indication abroad

c) Re-registration of expired geographical indications

d) Usage by non-authorized producers

11. Q. 93. Which section of Geographical Indications of Goods (Registration and Protection) Act, 1999 outlines the requirements for an application to register as an authorized user?

a) Section 12
b) Section 17
c) Section 23
d) Section 30

12. Q. 94. What is the Registrar's discretion regarding amendments under Section 15 of Geographical Indications of Goods (Registration and Protection) Act, 1999?

a) The Registrar can permit amendments only before advertisement
b) The Registrar can permit amendments only after the application is opposed
c) Amendments require judicial approval
d) The Registrar can permit correction of errors and amendments anytime, even after acceptance of an application

13. Q. 95. What is prohibited under Section 20(1) of Geographical Indications of Goods (Registration and Protection) Act, 1999?

a) Assignment of geographical indications
b) Renewal of geographical indications after expiry
c) Infringement proceedings for unregistered geographical indications
d) Appeal of Registrar's decisions

14. Q. 96. Under Section 26 of Geographical Indications of Goods (Registration and Protection) Act, 1999, what protection is granted to trade marks containing geographical indications?

a) It's validity cannot be challenged based on a GI registration if it was registered in good faith before the commencement of the Act
b) Automatic invalidation of a trade mark
c) No protection is granted to any kind of trade mark

d) Conditional protection to a trade mark for five years

15. Q. 97. What is the deadline for responding to deficiencies under rule 31 raised by the Registrar under Geographical Indications of Goods (Registration and Protection) Rules, 2002?

a) 15 days
b) 1 month
c) 6 months
d) 2 months

16. Q. 98. Who can apply for registration of a Geographical Indication?

a) Any individual or a company
b) Any association of persons or organization of producers representing interest of producers
c) Both a & b
d) All of the above

17. Q. 99. What happens when a geographical indication application contains goods from multiple classes but only one application fee is paid?

a) The application is rejected outright
b) The applicant must amend the application in order to restrict the goods to a single class
c) The Registrar automatically divides the application
d) The application is kept pending until the fee discrepancy is resolved

18. Q. 100. Which of the following statements is TRUE about the Geographical Indications of Goods (Registration and Protection) Act, 1999?

a) The particulars relating to the registration of the geographical indications shall be incorporated and form Part 'A' of the Register
b) The particulars relating to the registration of the authorised users shall be incorporated and form part of Part 'B' of the Register
c) The particulars relating to the registration of the geographical indications and the authorized users shall find place simultaneously in the

same part of the register.

d) Both a & b

Part B: Mini Question Bank

7.2. Sample Questions for Paper -I

Q1. An application for Registration Geographical Indication does not require to include ....

   a. Map of Geographical Origin
   b. Uniqueness
   c. List of members of consultative groups
   d. List of inspection body.

Q2. An application for registration of GI to be made in single application for different classes to filed in Form....

a. Form GI-1; Entry 1-A
b. Form GI-1; Entry 1-B
c. Form GI-1; Entry 1-C
d. Form GI-1; Entry 1-D

Q3. An application for registration of authorised user of a registered Geographical Indication is to be made in Form ....

a. Form GI-2
b. Form GI-5
c. Form GI-4
d. Form GI-3

Q4. Notice of opposition to the GI application which is advertised in Journal need to file within ....without seeking provision of extension.

a. 10 months
b. 4 months
c. 3 months

d. 12 months

Q5. Certificate of registration of geographical indication is issued by the Registrar in form ....

a. Form GI-10
b. Form O-2
c. Form O-5
d. Form GI-8

Q6. As per Rule 77, additional protection for the certain goods which are notified by the Central Government under sub-section (2) of Section 22; need to file in Form ....

a. Form GI-1
b. Form GI-2
c. Form GI-8
d. Form GI-9

Q7. Where an application for registration of geographical indication does not satisfy requirements under Section 11 or Rule 23, the Registrar shall send notice thereof to the applicant to remedy the deficiencies and if within...........month(s) from the date of receipt of notice, the applicant fail to remedy and deficiency so notified by him applicant may be treated as abandoned.

a. One month
b. Two months
c. Three Months
d. Four months

Q8. On receipt of an application for GI registration, the Registrar shall constitute a Consultative group of not more than ....representatives chaired by him from organisation or authority or person well versed in the varied intricacies of law or field.

a. Three
b. Ten

c. Six

d. Seven

Q9. The Registrar serves the notice of opposition for the Registration of GI to the applicant; the applicant shall send to the Registrar in the prescribed manner a counter statement based on the ground on which he relies for his application in Form ....within ...., if he does not do so, he shall be deemed to have abandoned his application.

a. Form GI-2; Four Months

b. Form GI-2: Two Months

c. Form GI-4: One month

d. Form GI-4: Two Months

Q10. Which of the following statement is wrong with respect to the 'Authorised user' of registered Geographical Indication?

a. Particulars relating to the registration of Authorised user the geographical indication shall be incorporated and form Part B of the register in the prescribed manner.

b. There is no need to renew the Registration of Authorised User

c. Registration of an authorised user shall be for 10 year if life of GI registration is valid for 10 years.

d. The registration of the authorised user expires on the date on which registration geographical Indication expires.

Q11. Which of the following statement is correct within the meaning of Geographical Indication of Goods (Registration and Protection) Act, 1999 and Rule 2002.

a. There is no difference in Trade Mark & Geographical Indication, both are registration of logo.

b. An interested person may request to refuse or invalidate the registration of Trade Mark which consist of geographical Indication under section 25 of the G.I. act.

c. The right obtained by virtue of GI registration is assignable/ transmissible.

d. There is no need to renew GI registration, it's for lifelong of the applicant.

Q12. If Karnataka State Handicrafts Development Corporation Limited is willing to file their Geographical indication in class 6, 21 and 34 in one application only, then the filing fees required to paid in INR .....

a. 5000/-
b. 4500/-
c. 15000/-
d. 13500/-

Q13. A textile association filed GI Registration application in class 24 and 25 which is accepted and advertised by the Registrar in the journal, a person interested is filing notice of opposition suggest him the fees required to pay for both the classes.......

a. 1000/-
b. 900/-
c. 2000/-
d. 1800/-

Q14. In above circumstances the fees required to be paid by textile association for filing counter statement is ....

a. 900/-
b. 2000/-
c. 1800/-
d. 1000/-

Q15. As per Rule 105, which of the following statement is wrong with respect to
non-eligibility for registration as a Geographical Indications Agent if he
....

a. is an undercharged insolvent
b. has been convicted by a competent court.
c. Has been adjudged by a competent Court to be of unsound mind
d. None of these

Answer key:

1-C ; 2-d; 3-d; 4-b; 5-b; 6-d; 7-a; 8-d; 9-b; 10-b; 11-b; 12-c; 13-c; 14-d; 15-d.

It is requested to go through the book again and possible questions are framed in the book at respective places with the running topic.

7.3. Sample Questions for Paper -II

Q.1. *XYZ association reached to you for filing of Geographical Indication for BC goods belonging to agriculture. Draft the Form for filing of same to the GI Registry.*

A.

To,

The Registrar of Geographical Indications

The office of Geographical Indications Registry, Chennai

Form GI-1

Application for the registration of a geographical indication in Part Aof the Register

Section 11(1), rule 23(2)

1. Application is hereby made by for the registration in Part A of the Register of the accompanying geographical indication furnishing following particulars;

Name of the applicant: XYZ association

Address: XYZ association, AB city , BD State, Pin Code: XXXXXX

List of association of persons/producers/ organisation/authority

Type of goods:

Specification:

Name of Geographical indication [and Particulars]:

Description of the goods:

Geographical area of production and map:

Proof of origin [Historical record]:

Method of production:

Uniqueness:

Inspection body:

Other:

Along with statement of case in class ......in respect of ....in the name of ....whose addres is ....who claims to represent the interest of the producers of the said goods to which geographical indication relates and which is in continuous use since in respect of the said goods.

2. the applicant shall include such other particulars called for in rule 32(1) in the statement case

i.e.

- statement as how the geogra[hical indication serves to designate the goods as originating from the concerned territory.
- The class
- Geographical Map
- Particulars regarding the appearance of GI comprising word or figurative element
- a statement containing particulars of producers
- Statement containing affidavit for said claim; standard benchmark for the use of GI; particular of mechanism; certified copies of the map; particulars of special human skill; full name and pariculars of association of person; particulars of the inspection structure as regulatory body; and material factors differentiating -in the case of homonymous indication.

3. All communication relating to this application may be sent to the following address in India.

....
Signatory
Name of Signatory (In Block Letter)

ᗡᗡᗡ

Q.2. If question for drafting opposition to the application for registration of Geographical Indication then following template can be used.

To,

The Registrar of Geographical Indications

The office of Geographical Indications Registry, Chennai

Form GI-2

Notice of opposition to application for registration of a geographical Indication

[Section 14(1), 17(3) ; rule 41(1)]

In the matter of application No................by................

I (or we) ....hereby give notice of my (or our) intension to oppose the registration of the geographical indication under above matter for class.... ....in the Geographical Indication Journal dated.........the day of ....no ....page....

The grounds for opposition are as follows:-

(You need to select one or more grounds based on situation provided in the question)

you can take help of following options:

- As per sec 9(a) said Geographical indication -use of which would likely to deceive or cause confusion.
- As per sec 9(b) said Geographical indication-the use of which would be contrary to any law for time being in force.
- As per sec 9(c) said Geographical indication- comprises or contain scandalous or obscene matter
- As per sec 9(d) said Geographical indication- matter likely to hurt the religious susseptibilities of any class or section of citizen of India.
- As per sec 9(e) said Geographical indication -which would otherwise be discentitled to protection in a court.
- As per sec 9(f) said Geographical indication- which are determined to be generic name or indications of goods and are therefore, not or ceased to be protected in their country of origin or which have fallen into disuse in that country.
- As per sec 9(f) said Geographical indication- which are determined to be generic names or indication of goods.
- As per sec 9(f) said Geographical indication-which is falsely representation of origin of GI.

I the undersigned do solemnly verify that the information provided here and the document furnished are true the level of my knowledge and obtained from the history of above-mentioned company.

Dated this... day of ... 20....

....
Signature (Applicant/Authorised Agent)

ᐯᐯᐯ

Q.3. If question is require to file Counterstatement.

To,

The Registrar of Geographical Indications

The office of Geographical Indications Registry, Chennai

Form GI-2

Form of Counterstatement

Sections 2, 14, 17(3), Rule 43(1), 66

In the matter of an opposition No..... to the application No.......in class ....for the registration of geographical indication.

I(we)...........the applicant(s) for registration of the above geographical indication, hereby give notice that the following are ground on which I/we rely for my application:

I(we) admit the following allegations in the notice of opposition.....

2. All communications in relation to the proceedings may be send ro the following address in India:

I the undersigned do solemnly verify that the information provided here and the document furnished are true the level of my knowledge and obtained from the history of above-mentioned company.

Dated this..................day of 20

....

Name of Signattory (In block letters)

Q.4. If any question demands drafting of affidavit with respect to GI matter, then following template can be used.

To,

The Registrar of Geographical Indications

The office of Geographical Indications Registry, Chennai

Affidavit is furnished as required

Form GI-7

(Entry No 7-B)

I,......................of ....do hereby solemnly and sincerely declare that the particulars set out in the statement of case, exhibit marked................and left by me in connection with ....in respect of the Geographical Indication No...............in class ....are true and comprise every material fact and doument affecting the present proprietorship of the geographical indication, to the best of my knowledge, information and belief.

Dated This.............of ......

Signature of deponent

Following things you need to mind when filling affidavit.

The affidavit -to be stamped under the law for the time being in force.

- Insert full name, address and nationality of deponent.
- Insert particulars of the proceeding concerned.
- To be signed here by the person making the declaration.
- Signature and title of authority before whome affidavit taken.

In India affidavit may be taken before any court or person having authority to receive evidence or before an officer empowered by a court or person having by law autjority to receive evidence or before an officer empowered by a court to administer oath.

For affidavit outside of India, oath may be taken before a Diplomatic or Consular Officer within the meaning of the Diplomatic and Consular Officer Act, 1948, of such country or place before a Notary of the place if the notorial act done by notaries of the place have been recognised by the Central Governmnt under sec 14 of the Notarises Act, 1952.

ᗕᗕᗕ

These are just sample example, more you cover the actual concepts more marks you will get, whatever may be the style/complexity of the qusetion.

Best of luck!!!

For refereing the concepts on Trade Mark Act and Rule; you may refer book "Concise Trade Mark Masterkey.'

ᗕᗕᗕ

Annexure I

Enlisting of
Sections of 'The Geographical Indication of Goods (Registration and Protection) Act, 1999'
&
Rules of 'The Geographical Indications of Goods (Registration and Protection) Rule, 2002

The Geographical Indication of Goods (Registration and Protection) Act, 1999

CHAPTER I: PRELIMINARY

Sec 1: Short title, extent and commencement
Sec 2: Definition and interpretation

CHAPTER II: THE REGISTER AND CONDITION FOR REGISTRATION

Sec 3: Registrar of Geographical Indications
Sec 4: Power of Registrar to withdraw or transfer cases, etc
Sec 5: Geographical Indication Registry and offices thereof
Sec 6: Register of Geographical Indications
Sec 7: Part A and Part B of the register
Sec 8: Registration to be in respect of particular goods and area
Sec 9: Prohibition of registration of certain geographical indication
Sec 10: Registration of homonymous geographical indication

CHAPTER III: PROCEDURE FOR DURATION OR REGISTRATION

Sec 11: Application for registration
Sec 12: Withdrawal of acceptance
Sec 13: Advertisement of application
Sec 14: Opposition to registration

Sec 15: Correction and amendment
Sec 16: Registration
Sec 17: Application for registration as authorised user
Sec 18: Duration, renewal, removal and restoration of registration
Sec 19: Effect of renewal, removal and restoration of registration

CHAPTER IV: EFFECT OF REGISTRATION

Sec 20: No action for infringement of unregistered geographical indications
Sec 21: Rights conferred by registration
Sec 22: Infringement or registered geographical indications
Sec 23: Registration to be prima facie evidence of validity
Sec 24: Prohibition of assignment or transmission

CHAPTER V: SPECIAL PROVISION RELATING TO TRADE MARK AND PRIOR USE

Sec 25: Prohibition of registration of geographical indication as trade mark
Sec 26: Protection to certain trade mark

CHAPTER VI: RECTIFICATION AND CORRECTION OF THE REGISTER

Sec 27: Power to cancel or vary registration and to rectify the register
Sec 28: Correction of register
Sec 29: Alternation of registered geographical indications
Sec 30: Adaptation of entries in register to amend or substitute classification of goods

CHAPTER VII: APPEALS

Sec 31: Appeals to HC
Sec 34: Procedure for application of rectification before HC
Sec 35: Appearance of Registrar in legal proceedings

CHAPTER VIII: OFFENCES PENALTIES AND PROCEDURE

Sec 37: Meaning of applying geographical indication

Sec 37-A: Adjunction of penalties

Sec 37-B: Appeal

Sec 38: Falsifying and falsely applying geographical indications

Sec 39: Penalty for applying false geographical indications

Sec 40: Penalty for selling goods to which false geographical indication is applied

Sec 41: Enhanced penalty on second or subsequent conviction

Sec 42: Penalty for falsely representing a geographical indication as registered

Sec 45: No offences in certain cases

Sec 46: Forfeiture of goods

Sec 47: Exemption of certain person employed in ordinary course business

Sec 48: Procedure where individuality of registration is pleaded by the accused

Sec 49: Offences by companies

Sec 50: Cognization of certain offence and powers of police officer for search and seizure

Sec 51: Cost of defence of prosecution

Sec 52: Limitation of prosecution

Sec 53: Information as to commission of offence

Sec 54: Punishment for abatement in India of act done out of India

CHAPTER IX: MISCELLANEOUS

Sec 55: Protection of action taken in good faith

Sec 56: Certain person to be Public servant

Sec 57: Stay of proceedings where the validity of registration of the geographical indication is questioned

Sec 58: Application for rectification of register to be made to HC in certain cases

Sec 59: Implied warranty on sale of indicated goods

Sec 60: Power of Registrar

Sec 61: Exercise of discretionary power by Registrar

Sec 62: Evidence before Registrar

Sec 63: Death of Party to a proceeding

Sec 64: Extension of time

THE GEOGRAPHICAL INDICATION OF GOODS (REGISTRATION AND PROTECTION) RULES, 2002

PART I

CHAPTER I

PRELIMINARY

Rule8: Document file or left not at the appropriate office

Rule9: Issue of notices

Rule10: Fees

Rule11: Forms

Rule12: Size of documents

Rule13: Signing of documents

Rule14: Services of documents

Rule15: Particulars of address of applicants and other persons

Rule16: Statement of principal place of business in India in an application

Rule 17: Address for service

Rule18: Address for service in application and opposition proceedings

Rule19: Non availability of an address for service

Rule 20: Agency

Rule21: Classification pf Goods

Rule 22: Request to registrar for search

CHAPTER II: PROCEDURE FOR REGSITRATION OF GEOGRAPHICAL INDICATION

Rule 23: Form and signing of application

Rule 24: Application under convention arrangement

Rule 25: Statement of user in application

Rule 26: Representation of geographical origin

Rule 27: Additional representation

Rule 28: Representation to be durable and satisfactory

Rule 29: Transliteration and translation

Rule 30: Name and description of goods on geographical indication

Rule 31: Deficiencies

Rule 32(1): Content of application

Rule 32(2): Acknowledgement of receipt of application

Rule 33: Examination of application

Rule 34: Objection of acceptance hearing

Rule 35: Decision of Registrar

Rule 36: Correction and amendment of application

Rule 37: Withdrawal of acceptance by the Registrar

Rule 38: Manner of advertisement

Rule 39: Notification of correction or amendment of application

CHAPTER III: AUTHORISED USER

CHAPTER IV: RENEWAL OF REGISTRATION AND RESORATION

CHAPTER V: RECTIFICATION AND CORRECTION OF REGISTER ALTERATION OR REACTIFICATION OF

REGISTER

Rule 65: Application to rectify or remove a GI from the register
Rule 66: Further proceedings
Rule 67: Intervention by third parties
Rule 68: Rectification of the register by the Registrar of his own motion
Rule 69: Alteration of address in the register
Rule 70: Application under section 28
Rule 71: Alteration of registered GI
Rule 72: Advertisement before decision and opposition
Rule 73: Decision -Advertisement-notification

CHAPTER VI: SPECIAL PROVISION RELATING TO TRADE MARKS

Rule 74: Refusal or invalidation of registration of TM
Rule 75: Refusal or invalidation of registered TM conflicting with a GI notified under sec 22(2)
Rule 76: Publication of or invalidation of GI

CHAPTER VII: PROCEDURE RELATING TO ADDITIONAL PROTECTION TO CERTAIN GOODS UNDER SEC 22(2) OF GI OF GOODS (REGISTRATION AND PROTECTION) ACT, 1999

Rule 77: Additional protection to certain goods
Rule 78: (joint application)
Rule 79: Consideration by the Registrar
Rule 80: Hearing before refusing an application
Rule 81: Entry in the register
Rule 82: (A) Single application
Rule 82(B): Divisional application
Rule 83: Extension of time
Rule 84: Exercise of discretionary Power of Register
Rule 85: Notification of decision
Rule 86: Amendment and correction of irregularity in procedure
Rule 87: Directions not otherwise prescribed
Rule 88: Hearing

PART II: REGISTRATION OF GEOGRAPHICAL INDICATIONS AGENT

References & Important Links

References

The Geographical Indication of Goods (Registration and Protection) Act, 1999

The Geographical Indications of Goods (Registration and Protection) Rule, 2002

The Trade Mark Act, 1999

The Trade Mark Rule, 2017

The Jan Vishwas (Amendment of Provisions) Act, 2023

Links:

www.ipindia.gov.in

https://nclpub.wipo.int/enfr/

Further Assistance

Reader of this book can reach to the author by these simple steps.

You need to just Type 'GImasterkey-1' on whats app no 7276120384 to get add in her core group.

Or email to her on email 'patentmasterkey@gmail.com.

<table>
<tr><td>Online Course provided by Author</td><td>Services provided by the Author</td></tr>
<tr><td>

- Training Course-Patent agent Exam
- Training of Patent Drafting
- Training course -Design Act & Rule
- Training course -Trade Mark Agent Exam
- Training course-Geographical Indication

</td><td>

- Patent search
- Patent Draft
- Patent Filing & Prosecution
- Filing & Prosecution of Design Application
- Trade Mark Filing
- Trade Mark pre-grant Opposition
- Attending Hearing in all IP matters

</td></tr>
</table>

Books helpful to Clear
<u>Patent Agent Exam</u>

Books helpful to Clear
<u>Trade Mark Agent
Exam</u>

Enter Caption

Best of luck!!
Keep on practice ....
Practice makes the success, obvious.....